DEVELOPING AN UNDERSTANDING OF WORLD PROBLEMS

DEVELOPING AN

WORLD

AN INTRODUCTION TO INTERNATIONAL LAW
BY CASE STUDIES

by

ROBERT M. STEPHEN
Chairman, Social Studies Department
Naperville Community High School
Naperville, Illinois 60540

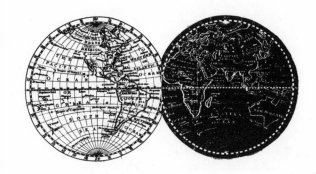

UNDERSTANDING
OF
PROBLEMS

1969
OCEANA PUBLICATIONS, INC.   Dobbs Ferry, New York

Manufactured in the United States of America

TABLE OF CONTENTS

PREFACE

The surging optimism of the Victorian Age, the period of Wilsonian idealism, and the post World War eras in the interpretation of international relations has been largely replaced at present by a somewhat skeptical and cynical state of mind. To wit, we have had manifestations of this intransigence at the domestic level in our own country; but, more importantly, at the international contact level this cynicism has projected itself by discounting the efficacy of law, ethics, and morality. The desire to continue to rely on maintaining a modicum of advantage in the highly competitive and costly arms race as a means of deterrence against potential aggression is most indicative of the state of mind existing at this time. The question then arises in the minds of men: Can the "balance of terror" provide our world community with the peaceful international climate and growth which we shall require to solve our lingering, present, and future problems? Confronted with this challenge, I was stimulated to seek a means by which this need for greater understanding by secondary students in the area of world relations could be achieved. This project is an attempt to attain that goal.

The primary assumption underlying this material is that, through the study of the topics and pertinent cases chosen, a most satisfactory method in developing understanding of world problems and a peaceful world community may be pursued and hopefully achieved. It must be understood that in this attempt there is a myriad of material available, but those topics and cases chosen were felt to be significant in creating an "awareness" and "desire" to enlarge interest in this broad and viable field.

In keeping with this primary assumption, the use of ethical, moral, and legal concepts became the locus or center for a starting point. The major concepts which are stressed in this selected material are as follows: (1) world interdependence, (2) recognition of the worth and dignity of the individual, (3) development of moral and spiritual values, (4) justice through law, and (5) achieving peace through constructive social change.

The project which I have been engaged in developing is the end product of many and varied contributions, such as time, space, money, ideas, critiques, understanding and cooperation. To those who in their own inimitable manner contributed to the ultimate achievement of this goal, I should like to acknowledge grateful thanks.

First of all, to Miss Betty Reardon, Associate Director of L.A.W.S. (Leadership and World Society) and those of the L.A.W.S. organization, a sincere thank-you for interest in my project, financial aid, and a very stimulating idea exchange conference held at Williamsburg, Virginia.

To the Board of Education, District #107, Naperville Community High School; Superintendent, Dr. Charles Landreth; Curriculum Director, Mr. Thayer Hill; Principal, Mr. Charles Mattka; and my fellow colleagues of the high school staff, particularly Mr. Kenneth Kruse—a feeling of deep indebtedness for their encouragement, aid, and cooperation.

To Dr. Eggert Giere, of North Central College, Naperville, many thanks for ·contributions of valuable background material, as well as helpful advice and guidance.

Dr. John Lee, Director of Project Social Studies, Northwestern University, deserves special mention for his very timely evaluation and critical comments concerning this embryonic project.

To Dr. Mark Krug and Dr. Paul Johnson of the University of Chicago, my appreciation for an extremely rewarding summer institute which provided a great deal of impetus and direction.

Lastly, to my wife, my gratitude for typing this material.

ROBERT M. STEPHEN, JR.
June 9, 1967
Naperville, Illinois 60540

TO THE STUDENT

Directions and the Problem

The responsibility of the student is to: (1) read, analyze, and master the material covered in the illustrative cases, the appendices as they relate to the case study or topic being studied, and the case studies assigned; (2) attempt through the inductive self-discovery method to determine topic-related cases and the issues involved which may be determined from the case facts presented and the decision rendered; (3) be prepared to brief an assigned case, to work and cooperate in a group, and to present his conclusions to the class, either in a formal presentation or through discussion in class; and (4) indicate a knowledgeable mastery of the study unit by written evaluation or examination.

TOPIC AREAS TO BE STUDIED

I. Illustrative Cases: (example)
  A. Topics and cases matched
    1. Nature, Definition, and Function of International Law
       The Lotus Case, 1927
    2. The Sources of International Law
       The Scotia, 1871
    3. International Law in Relation to Municipal Law
       Mortensen v. Peters, 1906
    4. Recognition of States and Governments
       Republic of China v. Merchants' Fire Assurance Co., 1929
II. Case Studies
  A. Cases to be matched with topics
    1. Nature, Definition, and Function of International Law

    2. Sources of International Law

    3. International Law in Relation to Municipal Law

    4. Recognition of States and Governments

    5. Continuity of States and State Succession

    6. Territory and Territorial Jurisdiction

    7. Jurisdiction in the High Seas

    8. Nationality and Jurisdiction over Nationals

    9. Extradition: Jurisdiction over Aliens

    10. Rights and Immunities of States in Foreign Courts

    11. International Responsibility for Damages to Aliens

    12. Status and Immunities of Diplomats and Consuls

ILLUSTRATIVE CASES

Part I
Definition, Nature, and Function
of International Law

OUTLINE OF CONTENT

A. Definition
 1. Regulation of relations between sovereign states by law (a traditional concept)
 2. Modern hypothesis: law also regulates relations between individuals with states and in some cases to certain interrelationships of individuals themselves *(see Jessup in Summary)

B. Nature
 1. Tradition of need and long historic evolution arose from custom, usage, agreements, treaties, principles of natural justice, ethics, and morality, based on the firm assumption these developments have been recognized by civilized states as being binding and obligatory. Obligations are stressed in International Law and thus procedural rights, remedies, and forceful executions of rules have been minimized
 2. Life is regulated by written and unwritten law.
    a. Law may be construed in a two-fold sense:
       (1) Rule or guide for human, group, or state behavior (obligations and substantive rights)
       (2) System of enforceable rules predicated on political arrangements (states) and having objective categories within these political entities (remedial and procedural in nature)

C. Function
 1. Ultimate purpose is peace, order, human well-being and justice in our troubled world

D. Identifications (see Appendices I and II)
 1. Terms, p. 130.
 2. People, p. 133.
 3. Time Chart Events, p. 111.
 4. Dissenting Opinion—*Lotus Case, 1927,* p. 129.

E. Illustrative Case Study
 1. *The Lotus Case, 1927*

1

F. Summary
1. Supplementary Background Readings
   *a. Jessup, *A Modern Law of Nations*, pp. 1-16 (esp. pp. 15 & 16).
   b. Fenwick, *International Law*, pp. 33-49.
   c. Stowell, *International Law*, pp. 3-26 (esp. p. 10).
   d. Lawrence, *Principles of International Law*, pp. 1-13.
   e. Kelsen, *Principles of International Law*, pp. 3-16 (2nd. Ed., 1966).
   f. Briggs, *The Law of Nations: Cases, Documents and Notes*, pp. 17-24.
   g. Corbett, *The Study of International Law*, pp. 1-10.
   h. Wright, *Contemporary International Law: A Balance Sheet*, pp. 1-12.
   i. Kaplan and deB. Katzenbach, *The Political Foundations of International Law*, pp. 3-82.
   j. Brierly, *The Law of Nations*, p. 53.

THE LOTUS CASE, 1927

Permanent Court of International Justice

On August 2, 1926, just before midnight, a collision occurred six miles out at sea. The *Boz-Kourt*, a Turkish collier, was cut in two by the French mail steamer *Lotus*, as the *Lotus* was proceeding through the Sea of Marmora to the port of Istanbul. The *Boz-Kourt* sank, and eight Turkish nationals who were on board perished. The *Lotus* did everything possible to rescue the shipwrecked persons, and ten were saved. The *Lotus* then continued on its course to Constantinople (Istanbul), arriving on August 3, 1926.

The same day the Turkish police proceeded to hold an inquiry into the collision on board the French mail steamer, the *Lotus*. Monsieur Demons, a French citizen, a lieutenant in the French merchant service, and first officer of the *Lotus*, was the officer of watch on board the *Lotus* at the time of the collision, which took place between five and six nautical miles to the north of Cape Sigri (Mitylene) in the Sea of Marmora. The following day, August 4, the captain of the *Lotus* handed in his master's report at the French Consulate-General, in Istanbul, transmitting at the same time a copy of his report to the harbor master of Istanbul.

On August 5, Lieutenant Demons was requested by the Turkish authorities to go ashore to give evidence, and he complied with the Turkish request. The examination led to the arrest of the Lieutenant — and Hassan Bey, the rescued captain of the *Boz-Kourt*. The length of the examination, incidentally, resulted in delaying the departure of the *Lotus*; and the arrest, characterized by the Turkish agent as arrest pending trial (*arrestation preventive*) was made without previous notice being given to the French Consul General. This arrest was effected to ensure that the criminal prosecution instituted against the two officers, Demons and Hassan Bey, should follow its normal course. The charge lodged against Lieutenant Demons and Hassan Bey was manslaughter, preferred by the Public Prosecutor of Stamboul, on the complaint of the families of the victims of the collision.

August 28 — The case was first heard by the Criminal Court of Stamboul. Lieutenant Demons submitted that the Turkish Courts had no jurisdiction. The Court overruled his objection.

Sept. 11 —Proceedings resumed. Lieutenant Demons demanded his release on bail.

Sept. 13 —Request for bail complied with; fixed at 6,000 Turkish Pounds.

Sept. 15 —Criminal Court delivered its judgement:

Lieutenant Demons was sentenced to 80 days' imprisonment and a fine of twenty-two pounds.

Hassan Bey received a slightly more severe penalty.

The Public Prosecutor of the Turkish Republic then entered an appeal against this decision, which had the effect of suspending its execution until a decision upon the appeal had been given.

The action of the Turkish judicial authorities with regard to Lieutenant Demons immediately brought protest from the French Government and its representatives in Turkey—diplomatic representations protesting his arrest, demanding his release or the transfer of the case from the Turkish Courts to the French Courts. As a result, the Government of the Turkish Republic declared on September 2, 1926, that "it would have no objection to the reference of the conflict of jurisdiction to the Court at The Hague".

The French Government fully consented to this proposed solution on September 6, and the two Governments appointed their plenipotentiaries to draw up a special agreement to be submitted to the Court. This was signed at Geneva on October 12, 1926, and the ratifications were deposited on December 27, 1926.

ISSUES: By a special agreement signed at Geneva on October 12th, 1926, between the Governments of the French and Turkish Republics and filed with the Registry of the Court, in accordance with Article 40 of the Statute and Article 35 of the Rules of Court, on January 4th, 1927, by the diplomatic representatives at the Hague of the aforesaid Governments, the latter have submitted to the Permanent Court of International Justice the question of jurisdiction which has arisen between them following upon the collision which occurred on August 2nd, 1926, between the steamships *Boz-Kourt* and *Lotus*.

According to the special agreement, the Court has to decide the following questions:

"(1) Has Turkey, contrary to Article 15 of the Convention of Lausanne of July 24th, 1923, respecting conditions of residence and business and jurisdiction, acted in conflict with the principles of international law—and if so, what principles—by instituting, following the collision which occurred on August 2nd, 1926, on the high seas between the French steamer *Lotus* and the Turkish steamer *Boz-Kourt* and upon the arrival of the French steamer at Constantinople—as well as against the captain of the Turkish steam-

4

ship—joint criminal proceedings in pursuance of Turkish law against M. Demons, officer of watch on board the *Lotus* at the time of the collision, in consequence of the loss of the *Boz-Kourt* having involved the death of eight Turkish sailors and passengers?"

"(2) Should the reply be in the affirmative, what pecuniary reparation is due to M. Demons, provided, according to the principles of international law, reparation should be made in similar cases?"

The Court decided question #1 in the negative. As a result of the negative decision pertaining to question #1, question #2 need not be answered. (See Appendices I and II for further information and a dissenting opinion concerning the case, pp. 111, 129, 130, and 133.)

Part II
Sources of International Law

THE SCOTIA, 1871

United States Supreme Court

This case was brought before the United States Supreme Court
on the basis of an appeal from the Circuit Court for the Southern
District of New York. It resulted from a case of collision off the
U. S. mainland between an American sailing ship, *Berkshire*, and
the British steamer, *Scotia*, which occurred in the main navigational
channel between the port of New York City and the British Isles.
In the ensuing collision the American sailing ship, *Berkshire*, was
sunk and totally lost. The owners of the *Berkshire*, a man named
Sears and his partners, on their own behalf, and also on behalf
of the owners of the cargo carried by the *Berkshire*, filed their libel
suit against the *Scotia* in the Southern District Court at New York,
to recover the losses sustained by the collision and the sinking of
the *Berkshire*. The libel suit charged that the collision occurred
through the fault of the British steamer, *Scotia*. The District Court
dismissed the *Berkshire's* libel suit, and the Circuit Court later
affirmed this decree. The appeal by the *Berkshire* to the Supreme
Court then ensued.

In recounting the facts which led to the unfortunate collision
and disposition of the case, the *Berkshire* was found to have been
an American sailing ship which belonged to our merchant marine,
and the *Scotia* a steamer in the British maritime service. Thus, the
municipal laws of either the United States or Great Britain would
not determine or govern the judging of the case, but the maritime
law (law of the seas) would be the means of arriving at a decision,
since the high seas had been the locale for the collision. Furthermore, aside from a conflict of municipal laws which might arise
since the ships flew different national flags, municipal law did not
have the power to project itself into the high seas area. The major
point of contention concerned itself with the indicator lights displayed by both ships, and the significance attached to the indicator
lights on both ships. It was from the erroneous use of indicator
lights by the *Berkshire*, and the wrong significance attached to the
use of the *Berkshire's* lights by the *Scotia* that the collision occurred.

As time had progressed, maritime law, through customs developed
by usage of the high seas and treaties negotiated, had evolved a

9

set of common rules or orders concerning the use of lights on a ship to indicate its type, location and size. In 1863 Great Britain, a leading maritime power, had passed in its Orders in Council enlarged rules for indicating the lights to be carried by a ship to interpret its type, location, and size. The United States Congress, by an act passed on April 29, 1864, substantiated the up-dated British Orders in Council rules for the indicator lights of vessels plying the high seas. Thus, the British and American maritime rules at this time were concurrent and alike in this problem area.

It was stated in the facts that the *Berkshire,* contrary to the British and American maritime rules covering indicator lights on a ship, had located on her anchor-stock deck only a bright white light. This, according to the maritime rules adopted, indicated to the *Scotia* that the *Berkshire* was a steamer and appeared to be perhaps four or five miles away, since the light would appear very low to the surface of the sea on deck. The correct method which should have been used by the *Berkshire* was to place red and green lights on her deck and masts, thus indicating a sailing ship and providing an easy means for locating her. As a result of the wrong indicator light displayed on the *Berkshire* and the miscalculation of the fast steamer, the *Scotia,* the tragic collision occurred with the ensuing case and appeal developing out of the collision.

The United States Supreme Court affirmed the decree of the lower Courts and dismissed the libel suit of the *Berkshire* with costs.

Part III
Subjects of International Law

OUTLINE OF CONTENT

A. *Subjects* of International Law evolve from the *Sources* of International Law
   1. *Custom* - Customary Law - habit - use - conduct
   2. *Treaties* - Procedural Law - Contract - law making (legislation)
   3. *General Principles* - Self-interest - consent - mutual benefits - morality, reason, and justice

B. *Subjects*
   1. *Sovereign States* (see Chapter II, Article 34, 1 of World Court Statute)
      a. *Nation - nation state* - nationalism - nation state system - sovereignty - national self-interest - national self-help
      b. *Elements of a state* - human and natural resources - government - territory - independence or sovereignty (internal and external) - location
      c. *Problem areas* - concept of sovereignty - recognition - isolation - participation and interdependence - concept of equality of states - neutrality - world community - peace, law, justice, security, and dignity of man
   2. *Dependent States*
      a. *Limited sovereignty* - protectorates - mandates - satellites - colonies - trusteeships - strategic areas and cities - U. N. specialized agencies (W.H.O., I.L.O., U.N.E.S.C.O., F.A.O., World Bank, etc.) - Vatican City - Monaco - Andorra - Red Cross
   3. *Exceptions to Sovereign and Dependent States*
      a. Revolutions - civil wars - national and international wars - outer space
      b. Soviets recognize only sovereign states and dependent nationalities
   4. *Individuals*
      a. Practice has incorporated the individual into International Law

11

b. *Ad hoc bodies* or *Tribunals* - U.N. specialized agencies, piracy, war criminals, human rights, injuries,
   (1) Treaty of Versailles, Articles 297 and 304
   (2) London 4 Power Agreement of August 8, 1945, Article 1
   (3) Charter for International Military Tribunal, Article 6—see Briggs, *op. cit.*, p. 96.
   (4) United Nations - *Bernadotte Case, 1949*
C. Summary
   1. Supplementary Background Readings
      a. Fenwick, *International Law*, pp. 83-102.
      b. Jessup, *A Modern Law of Nations*, pp. 15-41.
      c. Corbett, *The Study of International Law*, pp. 19-44.
      d. Kaplan and deB. Katzenback, *The Political Foundations of International Law*, pp. 83-228.
      e. Falk and Mendlovitz, *The Strategy of World Order, Vol. 2, International Law*, pp. 5-377.
      f. Briggs, *The Law of Nations: Cases, Documents and Notes*, pp. 65-71, and 85-98.
      g. Sohn, *Cases on United Nations Law*, pp. 249-270.
      h. Syatauw, *Decisions of the International Court of Justice*, pp. 168-173.
      i. Tondel, ed., *The Aftermath of Sabbatino*, pp. 1-64.
   2. Diagram, skeletal chart, and exerpts clarifying sections A and B of Part III.(See Appendix I   pp. 116, 117, 118, 119, and 120.)

Part IV
Relations of International Law
to Municipal Law

OUTLINE OF CONTENT

A. International Law's effectiveness is recognizant upon its relations with and to national law and national self-interest
   1. *Areas of conflict*
      a. Customary International Law may be at variance with a nation's domestic law
      b. Procedural International Law may be at variance with a national law
      c. Customary International Norms may conflict with a Nation's law or custom
   2. *Theoretic priority* of International Law based on old Anglo-Saxon doctrine of incorporation — Practice has tended to emasculate this concept by interpretation of the sovereign states and their amending it to suit their national self-interest
      a. *Doctrine of incorporation* has been adopted in a number of nation-state constitutions (for U. S. position see Federal Constitution, Article VI — Law of the Land, p. 120). However, we should refer to *Paquette Habana Case 1900*, Briggs, *Law of Nations*, pp. 31-32, for a synoptic U. S. practice in relation to constitutional theory, and the *Over the Top Case 1925*, Kelsen, *Principles of International Law*, pp. 421, 423, to complement the synthesis.
   3. At the present time, it can be assumed that International Law is commonly accepted as having priority over national law in different ways and degrees (see Constitutional Provisions excerpts after case studies).
   4. Directions to further improvement, acceptance, and codification of International Law
      a. Increased emphasis in education and public information - positive approach, not shortcomings
      b. International Law should be made the focal point around which national law and national legislation

13

should be implemented - avoid conflicts and strengthen all areas involved

    c. Conversely, national law and national legislation should be enacted to strengthen International Law

    d. Where precedence has not been established by custom or treaty, the general principles of civilized states should be the guideline for the national courts to follow

B. Illustrative Case Study

    1. *Mortensen v. Peters, 1906*

C. Summary

    1. Supplementary Background Readings

        a. Fenwick, *International Law*, pp. 76-80.

        b. Gould, *Introduction to International Law*, pp. 155-171.

        c. Kelsen, *Principles of International Law*, pp. 421, 423, and 566. (2nd Edition, 1966.)

        d. Briggs, *Law of Nations: Cases, Documents and Notes*, pp. 58-65.

    2. Diagram and skeletal chart with explanations of sections A and B of Part IV. (See Appendices I and II, pp. 120, 121, 122, 123, and 134.)

MORTENSEN v. PETERS, 1906

Great Britain, High Court of Justiciary of Scotland

In 1889 a Herring Fishery Act was enacted by Parliament, applying to Scotland, which prohibited trawl-fishing within 3 miles of
the low-tide water mark on any part of the coast of Scotland. Also,
included in this regulatory Herring Fishing Act was a port by-law
provision which authorized the Fishery Board of Control to see that
no beam or otter trawl-fishing methods were to be used within a
line drawn from Duncansby Head, Caithness, to Rattray Point,
Aberdeenshire. In 1892 the port regulatory by-law of 1889 was amended to specify the whole area encompassing Moray Firth (a narrow
arm of the sea), the distance from headland to headland across
Moray Firth being about 70 miles' distance.

As time progressed, a number of British-owned herring trawlers
began registering their vessels under the Norwegian flag so as to
circumvent and dodge the prohibitions of the Herring Fishery Act
of 1889—the amended regulatory by-law of 1892, and treaty agreements with other North Sea fishing powers. Trawling activities
were then resumed in the Moray Firth by these British-owned,
Norwegian-registered trawlers on the assumption that British statutes and regulatory laws had no application or effect to herring
trawlers flying foreign flags beyond the 3-mile limit established in
past International Law. To comply with the foreign Norwegian
registry, these British-owned trawlers employed with the title of
ship's master a national of Norway and a few Norwegian crew
members, although for all practical purposes the Norwegians were
only front men and British crews in reality operated the foreign-
registered trawlers. By 1905 about 30 of these so-called "pseudo-
foreign" trawlers were fishing in Moray Firth, and only two genuine
foreign trawlers were combing the area for fish cargoes.

Mortensen v. Peters was a test case of the extent of British jurisdiction to regulate and prohibit trawl fishing in Moray Firth, regardless of the nationality of the vessel or the offender in charge of
operations. Mortensen, the appellant, was a Danish national; the
trawler of which he was master was registered under the Norwegian
flag. Denmark had been, but Norway had not been, a signatory to
the North Sea Fisheries Convention and Treaty of 1883. Mortensen

had been charged with having broken the Herring Fishery Act of 1889 by otter-trawling within the regulatory provisions of the amended by-law of 1892, by not being outside the line designated from Duncansby Head, Caithness, to Rattray Point, Aberdeenshire, in Moray Firth. Mortensen was summoned to the Sheriff Court at Dornoch, Caithness, Scotland, where he was convicted of having violated the Herring Fishery Act of 1889, and the regulatory amendment of 1892.

Mortensen then appealed his conviction by the Sheriff Court to the High Court of Justiciary of Scotland, where his conviction was upheld and his appeal was dismissed. The decision was unanimous by the High Court.

NOTE: As a result of the unanimous decision rendered by the High Court in *Mortensen v. Peters*, foreign trawlers refrained from fishing in Moray Firth for almost a year. However, they did return to trawl-fishing in 1907; and six masters, all foreigners, of Norwegian-registered trawlers, were apprehended in Moray Firth and five of the masters were convicted and remanded to prison by the Sheriff Court of Elgin, Aberdeenshire, Scotland. Diplomatic protests then followed and were lodged by the Swedish and Norwegian Governments on behalf of the convicted men, which led the British Government to release the imprisoned men and consider repayment of their fines.

The Economic and Political considerations of this famous test case throw light upon the legal issues involved, as well as some of the aspects of the relation between international law and international politics. The trawl-fishing industry, even by 1906, had become very efficient and competitive, and each nation-state deeply involved in this type of enterprise sought fishing bank advantages at the other's expense. As the North Sea area became more and more depleted of available fish, trawl-fishing vessels had to seek new source areas for fish cargoes. Consequently, Great Britain, as well as other fishing powers in this commercial fishing enterprise area were confronted with making protective regulations effective in their own area on one hand to protect their own fishing interests and yet provide some opportunity and area of comity for interdependent commercial fishing operations by all the powers involved in trawl-fishing. Even today, we have cases emerging in the trawl-fishing industry, to wit, the *Red Crusader* case of 1961, involving Great Britain and Norway.

Part V
Recognition of
States and Governments

OUTLINE OF CONTENT

A. Definitions and Background
  1. *Recognition* means a formal declaration or acknowledgement by the government of an existing state that it intends to attach and confer responsible customary legal consequences to a set of facts which exist and thereby clothe those facts with status and sovereignty in varying degrees.
  2. *The State* is an intangible image of an organized group of individuals who live in a definite territory and are collectively responsible for the acts of their government to which they have conferred sovereign control to act on their behalf in external and internal relations.
  3. *The government* of a state is composed of individuals whose decisions are, by a legal definition, deemed to be those of the state and carry the concept of collective responsibility with them.
B. Beginning and Origin, Continuance, and End or Termination of States
  1. *Existence* of a state is a matter and question of fact, not of law. Existence of a state is evidenced by effective control over the elements of statehood, not on the basis of legitimacy.
     a. Elements of existence are as follows: 1) independence, 2) territory, 3) people, and 4) legal order. Institutions and boundaries may change within the state, but this does not interrupt its basic fact of existence or its continuity.
  2. *Means* by which territorial title may be acquired and sovereign control established over a state and government (two methods).
     a. Original means is by discovery, occupation, prescription (long acceptance of the fact of customary control), accretion (land added by forces of nature), and use of force to annex by conquest.
     b. Derivative means is by adjudication and by cession.

17

3. *End or Termination* of a State and the problems involved:
   a. Succession problems emerge when state ceases to exist.
     (1) Factors ending a state's existence
       (aa) complete loss of territory or people
       (bb) complete loss of legal order and the effectiveness of control
   b. Problems of succession and responsible recognition
     (1) Extent to which successor state will accept duties and obligations of predecessor state, externally and internally
     (2) Recognition of a new state or a new government by objective or subjective tests and explicit or implied acceptance
   c. Problems of belligerency and insurgency
     (1) *Belligerency* - by recognizing insurgents as belligerents provides state with basis for neutrality and application of laws of war and neutrality, as does recognition of belligerency alone.
     (2) *Insurgency* - by recognizing insurgency and insurgents, one provides them with international status, duties and obligations—it may also have a helpful effect.
     (3) Involvement in these two areas may be determined by the degree of recognition indicated and accepted, and the responsibility accepted by the states and their government.
   d. Problems of open intervention and occupancy are based on the concept that legal rights and obligations may be created by an illegal act; acceptance of responsibility becomes basis for recognition.

C. Factors and consequences growing from the grant or award of recognition
  1. Recognition confers the capacity to enter into legally and conclude international treaties as an equal among other equals.
  2. It provides for the ability to enter into diplomatic relations with other states.
  3. It retroactively ensures validity of acts and transactions of a state's government from the time when that state's government assumed power.
  4. It confers the right for a recognized state to appear as a plaintiff and appear before the courts of the state granting recognition.

5. Where state existence has had continuity, the treaty obligations of its predecessor usually devolve upon the newly recognized government and are considered to be binding.
6. The property and assets of a terminated government may be gained by a new government of the existing state within a recognizing state when recognition is granted by that state to the new government.
7. Insurgents who are recognized are granted limited international status, duties and obligations.
8. Belligerency which is recognized involves the implementation and application of the laws of war and neutrality to international and civil wars.

D. Illustrative Case Study
   1. *Republic of China v. Merchants' Fire Assurance Corporation of New York, 1929*

E. Summary
   1. Supplementary background readings are as follows:
      a. Fenwick, *International Law*, pp. 103-122.
      b. Stowell, *International Law*, pp. 37-48.
      c. Gould, *Introduction to International Law*, pp. 213-258.
      d. Kaplan and deB. Katzenbach, *The Political Foundations of International Law*, pp. 109-135.
      e. Briggs, *The Law of Nations: Cases, Documents and Notes*, pp. 99-238.
   2. Please see skeletal diagrams and identifications in Appendices I and II for supplementary background enlargement of recognition and its attendant problems, pp. 124, 125, 126, and 137.

REPUBLIC of CHINA v. MERCHANTS' FIRE ASSURANCE CORPORATION of NEW YORK, 1929

United States, Circuit Court of Appeals, Ninth Circuit

This case resulted from an appeal from the United States Court for China where the plaintiff, the Republic of China, had brought action by claiming damages against the Merchants' Fire Assurance Corporation of New York and against the Great American Insurance Company, New York. The United States Court for China had dismissed the claims of the plaintiff, the Republic of China, and the plaintiff then had carried their appeal to the United States Circuit Court of Appeals for review.

In recounting the background facts, the Republic of China had initiated an action in the United States Court for China to recover damages resulting from a fire loss under a policy which had been issued by the Merchants' Fire Assurance Corporation of New York to the Telephone Administration of the Chinese Government at Wuchang, China. The Telephone Administration was a department of the Republic of China, and the building plus the property which they had been using was covered by the policy issued prior to the very damaging fire. After the issuance of the covering policy and the later damaging fire, the armies of the national government (Kuomingtang) captured the city of Wuchang and thus became the custodian of the insurance policy and the property covered by the policy. When this action was initiated, the National Government was in control of 15 of the 18 provinces in China, which comprised about three-fourths of the total area of China proper, but the National Government of China had not been recognized by the United States. Thus, the defendant (insurance company) alleged before the United States Court for China that the plaintiff was not the Republic of China and filed a plea in abatement on this basis, and further stated that the new incumbent government was a revolutionary institution known as the National Government of China. Consequently, this new, revolutionary government was unrecognized by the United States of America, and as a result of this non-recognized status the National Government of China was without legal capacity to sue. The United States Court for China sustained the plea in abatement and dismissed judgement. The appeal by the plaintiff was then carried to the United States Circuit Court of Appeals, Ninth Circuit, and heard.

At the time of the trial in the lower court, the National Government of China had not been recognized by the United States, and it would seem to follow logically then that the new government in China was incapable of initiating a legal suit, since that new government had no recognized existence in contemplation of law. The courts in the United States are unable to recognize the existence of a government which originates in revolution, revolt, or coup, until that new entity has first been duly recognized by the political (executive and legislative) departments of the government. However, since the first trial in the lower court, much has changed in the interior concerning the question of recognition and legal capabilities of the new government in China. This court must now take heed and judicial notice of the changed circumstances in the plaintiff's appeal.

On July 25, 1928, an appointed representative (called an Envoy Extraordinary and Minister Plenipotentiary to China) by the President of the United States (Coolidge) met with the new Minister of Finance, appointed by the new National Government of the Republic of China. The two legally and duly accredited representatives of China and the United States then proceeded to enter into a treaty of commerce binding both powers with legal obligations. While this treaty has not yet been ratified by the U. S. Senate, clear recognition is implied and extended by our Executive Department to the new Chinese government and its accredited representative. Also, the new National Government of China has officially received our accredited envoy, and our Secretary of State (Kellogg) has verified this by telegram to the court.

The judgement of the lower court must, therefore, be reversed and the plaintiff's claims recognized.

CASE STUDIES

REGINA v. LESLIE, 1860

Great Britain, Court of Criminal Appeal

The prisoner being charged was the master (Captain Leslie) of the British vessel, *Louisa Braginton*. The charge against Captain Leslie was for false and improper imprisonment of a number of Chilean subjects who had been carried by Captain Leslie on the *Louisa Braginton* from Valparaiso, Chile, to Liverpool, England.

In recounting the facts, the government of Chile had ordered these Chilean subjects to be banished from Chile for activities which were termed seditious to their government. These rebellious people had been brought to the master (Leslie) of the *Louisa Braginton* under forceful circumstances. These so-called rebels had been guarded by Chilean regular soldiers and placed on board the English vessel by them. The representatives of the Chilean government and the master of the *Louisa Braginton* then consumated the contract which had been formulated between these two parties by conveying these banished and so-called rebellious Chilean subjects to Liverpool, England. Upon the arrival of the vessel, *Louisa Braginton*, at Liverpool, England, its master, Captain Leslie, and present defendant was summarily convicted of the above charges and imprisoned by the Order of the Liverpool Admiralty Court at the Christmas Assizes (court sessions). Captain Leslie appealed the decision to the Court of Criminal Appeals on the basis that the court at Liverpool did not have jurisdiction. The Crown (*Regina* - Queen Victoria), in presenting its side of the case against the defendant, Captain Leslie, and his appeal before the High Court of Criminal Appeal, Great Britain, stated that two questions must be answered with regard to Leslie's conviction and his subsequent appeal. First, can Leslie's conviction be upheld for that act which was done in Chilean waters? Second, can Leslie's conviction be sustained and his appeal dismissed for that which was done out of the Chilean jurisdiction and territory? The answer to the first question is no. The plaintiff (*Regina*) held that the Chilean government and state could act in its sovereign lawful capacity as it saw fit in its own territorial jurisdiction, and the act of Captain Leslie was also justified under those circumstances in that territorial context. However, the plaintiff, *Regina*, stated that in answer to the second question, the conviction of Captain Leslie by the lower court could be sustained on the basis that an English ship on the high seas, out of any foreign territory, is subject to the laws of England. Also, that any person or persons, whether they are English or foreign, on board an English ship are as much amenable and subject to English law as they would be on English soil. The court then cited the Merchant Shipping Act which was a statute in effect at that time that makes the master and seamen of a British ship responsible for all offenses against property or person committed on the high seas and out of Her Majesty's (*Regina*) dominions. The crime on board ship differed in no way with the jurisdiction and legal implications of a crime committed in England, and the Admiralty of England had prime jurisdiction. Thus, according to the law, Captain Leslie was involved in an act of false imprisonment, and he was therefore liable to conviction. A Chilean ship with Chilean subjects could have transported the banished Chileans to England, but not an English ship under the circumstances cited.

Conviction was affirmed and the appeal dismissed.

NIKITSCHENKOFF CASE, 1865

France, Criminal Court

This case arose in Paris, France, where a Russian subject by the name of Nikitschenkoff entered the Embassy of the Russian Empire in Paris and made a series of violent and murderous assaults upon the First Secretary of the Russian Embassy, and several foreign servants or domestics who had come to the assistance of the beleagued First Secretary. At the request of the First Secretary, the French police came into the Embassy and arrested the Russian subject, Nikitschenkoff. Shortly thereafter, the home Russian government demanded that the French deliver Nikitschenkoff for trial in Russia on the grounds that the French courts lacked jurisdiction over acts perpetrated· and committed on Russian soil. (Concept of extraterritoriality and comity were advanced.) The Russian Embassy and the soil on which it stands are not part of France nor under its jurisdiction, but are in reality part of Russia. The present case arose from the conflict of jurisdiction and who would hold and make Nikitschenkoff stand trial. Russia finally accepted concurrent jurisdiction in the case with France on the basis that the French police had been invited in by the Russian First Secretary of their embassy to restore order. Thus, the First Secretary had represented Russian interests in case and provided the French with jurisdiction.

Nikitschenkoff was tried and convicted of attempted murder and assault by the French Criminal Court. Russia concurred.

NOTE: Article 3 of the Code Napoleon states "all those who live in the territory (France) are subject to (French) police and security laws."

REGINA v. ANDERSON, 1868

Great Britain, Court of Criminal Appeal

James Anderson, an American citizen, employed as a seaman on a Canadian vessel, was indicted for the murder of a shipmate. The Canadian vessel was sailing under the Union Jack (British flag), registered in London, and owned by the port city of Yarmouth, Nova Scotia, Canada. The murder for which Anderson was indicted had been committed when the vessel was located about 45 miles inland on the Garonne River in the 2nd French Empire of Napoleon III, and the vessel had been proceeding on her way to her port of call, the French city of Bordeaux. The city of Bordeaux is located on the Garonne River about 90 miles inland from the Bay of Biscay. The point at which the murder took place in the Garonne River was at a location where the river was over ½ mile in width, and the vessel was positioned approximately 300 yards from the nearest shore. Also, the tide ebbs and flows up to and beyond the location spot of the murder, but no evidence was introduced as to whether the location of the ship at the time of the murder was or was not within the limits of the port of Bordeaux and its jurisdiction. At the October sessions of the Central Criminal, 1868, Anderson was convicted of manslaughter. Anderson immediately entered a petition of appeal to the higher Court of Criminal Appeal for a review of his manslaughter conviction and a dismissal of it on the basis that the lower court had no jurisdiction to try him.

The Crown (*Regina* - Queen Victoria), in presenting its side of the case against Anderson, based its position of sustaining the manslaughter conviction on the following arguments: The plaintiff stated that the crime had been committed within French territory and that Anderson was subject to the laws of France, if the French authorities had been so minded. But it was also true that the crime had been committed on a British merchant vessel, which at that time had been clothed with the protection of the British flag and British law, and was therefore subject to British law and its provisions. True, the prisoner was an American citizen, but by his own free will and consent he had embarked as a crew member on a British vessel and became subject to British law as a result of this decision. French custom, in dealing with offenses committed on

26

board foreign vessels within French territorial jurisdiction, has been not to assert police law unless the master of the ship requests it; or only when the peace and tranquility of the area has been disturbed will the French invoke their jurisdiction. Thus, it may be stated that the French, by not claiming concurrent jurisdiction, have given tacit approval to the English action, and America has long determined that they have jurisdiction over their vessels and their crews in foreign port, regardless of the crew member's nationality. General law and custom are sufficient to decide the case before this high court of appeal. A British ship is like a floating island; and, when a crime is committed on board a British ship, English law is amenable.

The High Court ordered the conviction of James Anderson affirmed and dismissed his appeal.

FONG YUE TING v. UNITED STATES, 1893

United States Supreme Court

This case developed upon the basis of three appeals from the Circuit Court of the United States for the Southern District of New York.

Originally, three Chinese laborers were arrested and held for deportation (return to China) by the marshall of this Southern New York District because they did not have certificates of residence as required by section 6 of the statute passed on May 5, 1892, New York State, and enforced by the collector of Internal Revenue in that stated area.

The appeal petitioner, Fong Yue Ting, and his two fellow petitioners who were in similar circumstances, alleged that he, Fong Yue Ting, was a member of the Chinese race (Mongoloid or Yellow race), born in China, and that he was not a naturalized American citizen. He further stated that in 1879 he had come to the United States with the intention of establishing residency here and remaining in this country, and that he had no desire or intention of returning to China. He also continued that since 1879 he had been a permanent resident of the United States, and that for over a period of a year had been located and had resided in the city and state of New York within the second district of said state for the collection of internal revenue. Furthermore, the petitioner stated that he had not, since the passage of the aforementioned statute of May 5, 1892, applied to the collector of internal revenue for said district for a certificate of residence, as required by section 6 of the state statute, and that he had always been without such a required certificate of residence. Fong concluded that he had been arrested by the marshall who claimed to do so under section 6 of the stated statute, and the marshall had performed this act without any writ or warrant.

The marshall, in his return to Fong's allegations, stated that Fong Yue Ting, the petitioner, had been found by him within the jurisdiction of the United States, in the stated Southern District of New York, and that the petitioner did not have the required certificate of residency for the area indicated. Therefore, in his capacity as marshall, he had arrested Fong Yue Ting and sought to bring him before a United States judge for the purpose of ascertaining specific facts and a course of action to pursue with regard to the petitioner. The marshall indicated that the petitioner, by means of questions put through an interpreter, had admitted to him (the marshall) that he was a Chinese laborer and that he was without the required certificate of residence.

The Circuit Court of the United States for the Southern District of New York, after a hearing upon the writ of *habeas corpus* (a writ for the purpose of bringing a party before a court or judge) and the marshall's return of his actions, dismissed the *habeas corpus* writ, admitted bail to those laborers involved, and allowed the petitioners the final appeal to the U. S. Supreme Court for decision.

The United States Supreme Court upheld the judgement of the Circuit Court, dismissing the writ of *habeas corpus*, and affirmed the judgement.

HILTON v. GUYOT, 1895

United States Supreme Court

This case reached the United States Supreme Court in error to and on appeal from the Circuit Court of the United States for the Southern District of New York.

Guyot had been appointed as the official liquidator of the French business firm, Fortin and Company. He initiated suit against Hilton and Libbey, U. S. citizens who had been trading as business partners in Paris and in New York. The action was brought in the United States Supreme Court for the Southern District of New York. Guyot's basis for the suit was a judgement which he had been awarded in Paris by the Tribunal of Commerce, a French court constituted and having jurisdiction over suits between merchants. In Paris the defendants, Hilton and Libbey, had appeared and counterclaimed against Guyot in the French court, but the judgement had been rendered against them and was further affirmed by the Court of Appeals in Paris. Prior to the judgement on appeal to the French Court of Appeals, Hilton and Libbey had liquidated their French business properties and stock; and, consequently, when judgement had been awarded and upheld by the French courts to Guyot, there was no property or collateral in the French jurisdiction out of which the judgement could be satisfied. As a result of not being able to execute the French judgement, Guyot brought action against Hilton and Libbey in the U.S. Circuit Court for the Southern District of New York; and, subsequently, from that court both Hilton and Libbey, on a writ of error and appeal, brought the case to the U.S. Supreme Court.

The Circuit Court directed a verdict for Guyot in the sum of $277,775.44, this being the amount of the French judgement plus interest. The United States Supreme Court reversed the judgement of the French Court of Cassation and the United States Circuit Court; remanded the case to the Circuit Court with a direction to set aside the award $277,775.44 and verdict and to order a new trial which would have a sound basis in the action at law and in the suit in equity. The French Court judgement was not to be considered as a bar to the new case.

UNDERHILL v. HERNANDEZ, 1897

United States Supreme Court

Early in 1892 a revolution erupted in Venezuela which the existing government in power failed to suppress. Subsequently, both the revolutionaries and the existing government in Venezuela claimed to be the one and only legitimate government for the nation-state of Venezuela. This case arose as a result of the fluctuating and changing conditions which emerged due to the ensuing civil war.

The existing government recognized as its head, Palacio; and the revolutionaries recognized as their leader, Crespo. General Hernandez belonged to the Crespo revolutionary group and was the commander of the revolutionary forces in the vicinity of Ciudad Bolivar, Venezuela. On August 8, 1892, Hernandez' revolutionary forces engaged the Palacio government forces some seven miles from Ciudad Bolivar; Hernandez and his troops won a smashing victory over the Palacio government forces. On August 13, 1892, Hernandez and his revolutionaries entered Ciudad Bolivar, and he assumed command and control of that area. The local government officials having fled prior to the occupation of Ciudad Bolivar, Hernandez immediately appointed from his own forces men to fill the vacant local positions. It was during this early Hernandez occupation that the major complaints resulted, as stated by Underhill in his ensuing petition. Later, by October 6, 1892, the Crespo revolutionaries had achieved success, and on October 23, 1892, the so-called "Crespo government" was formally recognized as the legitimate government of Venezuela by the United States.

Recounting some of the past facts: George F. Underhill was a citizen of the United States. He had constructed for the Palacio government under contract a waterworks system for Ciudad Bolivar, and he was engaged in supplying the city with water and operating the waterworks. Underhill also carried on a machinery repair business in Bolivar. A short time after General Hernandez' victory and occupation of Bolivar, Underhill applied to General Hernandez, as commanding officer, for a passport to enable Underhill to leave Ciudad Bolivar. Hernandez refused this request, as well as subsequent requests made by Underhill and some of his friends on his behalf; finally, on October 18, a passport was issued by Hernandez to Underhill, who promptly left Venezuela and returned to the U. S. A..

This action was then initiated by Underhill to recover damages for the detention caused by Hernandez and his refusal to grant Underhill a passport. Furthermore, Underhill alleged that he had been confined to his house and had been subjected to assaults and affronts by Hernandez' Army.

The case was first tried in the Circuit Court of the United States for the Eastern District of New York. The Circuit Court ruled on the conclusion of the plaintiff's case that, upon the facts presented, the plaintiff was not entitled to recover damages and directed a verdict in favor of the defendant, Hernandez. The Court used as its basis for grounds ruling in favor of Hernandez that "because the acts of the defendant were those of a military commander, representing a *de facto* government in the prosecution of a war, he was not civilly responsible".

The judgment having been rendered in the defendant's favor, the case was then taken to the Circuit Court of Appeals, and the verdict was reaffirmed by that Court upon the ground "that the acts of the defendant were the acts of the Government of Venezuela and as such are not properly the subject of adjudication in the courts of another government".

The United States Supreme Court upheld and agreed with the Circuit Court and the Circuit Court of Appeals that "the evidence upon the trial indicated that the purpose of the defendant in his treatment of the plaintiff was to coerce the plaintiff to operate his waterworks and his repair works for the benefit of the community and the revolutionary forces" and that " it was not sufficient to have warranted a finding by the jury that the defendant was actuated by malice or any personal or private motive". The Supreme Court concurred with the lower courts. The Supreme Court affirmed the decrees of the lower courts.

THE PAQUETTE HABANA, THE LOLA, 1900

United States Supreme Court

This case was heard and decided by the United States Supreme Court upon two appeals from decrees of the District Court of the United States for the Southern District of Florida, which had condemned the two fishing vessels, *Paquette Habana* and *Lola*, and the cargoes of the two vessels as prizes of war.

Both the *Paquette Habana* and the *Lola* were fishing smacks which made their home port at Havana, Cuba. They had regularly plied their trade to and from Havana and had consistently been engaged in the fishing industry off the Cuban coast, in fishing banks which were located adjacent to the Cuban territorial fishing waters. The two fishing smacks had sailed under the Spanish flag and were owned by Spanish subjects of Cuban birth. Both of the owners were permanent residents of the city of Havana, Cuba. The captains, or masters, employed by the owners of the two fish-·ing smacks were also Spanish subjects and residents of Havana, Cuba. The two masters and crews had no interest or equity in the two fishing vessels, but their compensation was earned on the basis of shares awarded according to the position occupied by master and crew member. In total shares awarded, the masters and crews of the two fishing vessels were entitled by their shares to two-thirds of the catch brought to port; the other one-third of the catch belonged to the two owners who owned the vessels outright. The cargoes of the fishing smacks consisted of fresh fish which had been caught by their crews from the high seas near Cuba. The fresh fish, as they were caught, were hauled aboard the fishing smacks, preserved and kept in cargo holds; and ultimately the catch was sold alive when delivered to purchasers at Havana. The *Paquette Habana* and the *Lola* had subsequently been stopped by an American blockading squadron during the Spanish-American War, and both fishing vessels had been brought by their American captors into Key West, Florida. Later, at Key West a libel for the condemnation of each vessel and each of their cargoes as a prize of war was filed on April 27, 1898, by the authorities in that area. With the filing of the libel for condemnation of the fishing smacks as prizes of war, a counter-claim was interposed concurrently by the masters of the fishing

33

smacks on behalf of themselves, their crews, and the owners of the two vessels. During the court proceedings, evidence was taken, showing the previously-stated facts and evolvements. On May 30, 1898, a final decree of condemnation and sale was entered by the District Court. The Court concluded that the "court not being satisfied that as a matter of law, without any ordinance, treaty or proclamation, fishing vessels of this class are exempt from seizure". The District then proceeded to initiate condemnation and sale proceedings, and appeal action was instituted by the owners and crew. The condemnation and sale decree of the District Court in Southern Florida was then brought by appeal to the United States Supreme Court by the masters of the *Paquette Habana* and the *Lola* who contended that, through ancient usage and custom among civilized nations, from past ages to the present, a rule of international law had developed whereby coast fishing vessels, which were pursuing their vocation of catching and bringing in fresh fish, have been recognized as exempt, along with their crews and cargoes, from capture as prizes of war. Furthermore, they stated that, when they had been stopped by the American blockading squadron, they had no knowledge of the existence of a war between Spain and the United States or of any blockade, for that matter. The masters also said that no arms or ammunition had been found on board the vessels, nor had they demonstrated any hostility, resistance, or made any attempt to run from the blockading American squadron at the time of their capture.

The United States Supreme Court heard the case.

The Court then recited that International Law is part of our law and must be ascertained and administered by the courts of justice of appropriate jurisdiction, as often as questions of right depending upon it are duly presented for their determination. For this purpose, where there is no treaty and no controlling executive or legislative act or judicial decision, resort must be made to the customs and usages of civilized nations; and, as evidence of these, to the work of learned jurists and commentators, who by years of labor, research, and experience, have made themselves well acquainted with the subjects of which they treat. Such works are resorted to by judicial tribunals, not for the speculations of their authors concerning what the law ought to be, but for trustworthy evidence of what the law really is.

The Court, after citing numerous sources and examples of past custom and usage in this field, concluded that, by the general consent of the civilized nations of the world, and independently of any express treaty or other public act, it is an established rule

34

of international law, founded on considerations of humanity to a poor and industrious order of men and of the mutual convenience of belligerent States, that coast fishing vessels, with their implements and supplies, cargoes and crews, unarmed, and honestly pursuing their peaceful calling of catching and bringing in fresh fish, are exempt from capture as prizes of war.

The Supreme Court then adjudged and declared that the capture was unlawful and without probable cause, and ordered that the decree of the District Court be reversed and the proceeds of the sale of the vessel, together with the proceeds of any sale of her cargo, be restored to the claimants (owners and crew members), with damages and costs to be added.

AMERICAN BANANA CO. v. UNITED FRUIT CO., 1909

United States Supreme Court

This action was brought about by the American Banana Company, the plaintiff, to recover triple damages from the United Fruit Company, the defendant, under the application of the Sherman Anti-Trust Act which sought to protect trade against monopolies. The original complaint had been dismissed by the lower federal Circuit Court of New Jersey, and their judgment had been upheld by their Circuit Court of Appeals of New Jersey. The case was then brought to the Supreme Court of the United States by writ of error.

The allegations of the complaint as lodged by the plaintiff may be summed up as follows: The American Banana Company, the plaintiff, was an Alabama corporation organized in 1904. The United Fruit Company, the defendant, was a New Jersey corporation organized in 1899. Quite some time prior to the formation and incorporation of the plaintiff as an active business organization, the defendant corporation had sought with premeditation, plan, and intent to prevent competition and to control and monopolize the banana trade. With this purpose in mind, the defendant corporation had bought the property and the business of several of its previous competitors. Included in some purchase provisions of their competitors were restraints against their former competitors resuming the banana trade. The defendant with other competitors had made contracts which regulated the quantity of bananas to be purchased, the price to be paid; and in still other competitors they had acquired a controlling amount of voting stock to enable them to manipulate the business to their own interests. Furthermore, the defendant had continued their original purpose by having organized a selling company or a trust company, of which it held and issued stock, and by agreement sold at fixed prices all the bananas of the combining parties. Thus, by this and other means the defendant did monopolize and restrain the banana trade, and prices were forced and unreasonable as a result of these carefully planned goals and built-in controls.

It was into this carefully controlled business area that J. McConnell, an American citizen, in 1903 began establishing a banana plantation in northern Panama, then a part of the United States of Colombia. To aid in exporting his bananas, McConnell began construction of a railway to port facilities on the Caribbean coast with the approval of and in accordance with Colombian laws. This railway would run very close to the border line of Costa Rica, and it was from this location that problems arose for McConnell. First, the defendant notified McConnell that he must either combine with them or stop his business development. McConnell flatly refused to heed the defendant's requests.

Several months later, it is believed at the defendant's request and instigation, the governor of Panama recommended to his Colombian government that the government of Costa Rica be allowed to administer the territory through which McConnell's railroad was to run to the sea even though this territory had been previously awarded to Colombia under an arbitration agreed to by treaty with Costa Rica. Shortly thereafter, McConnell was interfered with by the Costa Rican officials under inducement from the defendant.

In November 1903, Panama revolted and became an independent republic, declaring the Panamanian boundary to be that encompassing the earlier agreed to treaty. In June of 1904 the American Banana Company, the plaintiff, bought out the partially developed McConnell plantation and railroad, and went on with the work of completion and full development under the laws of the Republic of Panama. In July soldiers and officials from Costa Rica, under inducement again from the defendant, seized part of the plantation, needed supplies for construction, and prevented further construction and operation of the railroad. In August, J. Astua, a Costa Rican by *exparte* (on behalf of) proceedings, got a judgment from a Costa Rican court declaring the plantation to be his and in turn immediately sold the plantation to the defendant (United Fruit Co.).

The plaintiff had tried to persuade the Costa Rican government to withdraw its soldiers and had asked the United States to aid them. Due to actions by the defendant, the plaintiff had been thwarted in both attempts to seek justice and equity. The government of Costa Rica had remained in possession and occupation of the area up to the present hearing.

As a result of the defendant's actions, the plaintiff had been deprived of the use of the plantation and the railway. This had resulted in loss and injuries to the plantation, railway, and needed supplies. The defendant, by outbidding, had driven prospective purchasers from the market and prevented the plaintiff from normal business in export and sale of bananas. Last, but not least, the defendant had offered positions to the employees of the plaintiff which were damaging to the plaintiff's operation.

The plaintiff realized that the damaging acts were committed outside the jurisdiction of the United States, yet the plaintiff argued that, due to the wrongful business conspiracy involved, the situation should be governed by the act of Congress; namely, the Sherman Anti-Trust Act of July 2, 1890.

The Supreme Court observed that the plaintiff's case depended upon several unusual propositions. In the first place, the acts causing the damage were done, so far as appears from the facts, outside the jurisdiction of the United States and occurred within that of other states. The Court was surprised to hear it argued that they were governed by an act of Congress.

The Supreme Court affirmed the judgment of the lower courts and dismissed the complaint. (See Appendices I and II for further information.)

THE GAGARA, 1919

Great Britain, Court of Appeal

This case emerged from a lower Admiralty Court by appeal of the plaintiffs, the West Russian Steamship Company, Limited. The lower Admiralty Court had dismissed a writ *in rem* (action against a thing, rather than a person) and all subsequent proceedings against the steamship, *Gagara*, by the plaintiffs. The plaintiffs then appealed to this court.

In recounting the facts they evolved as follows: On January 1, 1919, the plaintiffs, the West Russian Steamship Company, Limited, procured from the lower Admiralty Court and served a writ *in rem* against the steamship *Gagara*, docked at London, which on the date stated above was now sailing under the name of the *Kajak*, and the group (the Esthonian Government) was now operating the former *Gagara* under the new name, *Kajak*. The plaintiffs stated in their filed affidavits, which led to a warrant of arrest to be issued, that they (the plaintiffs) were a lawful and legal corporate body with their main office located in the city of Petrograd (now Leningrad, U. S. S. R.) and that they (the plaintiffs) were duly registered in that city. Furthermore, they contended that they (the plaintiffs) were the true and lawful owners of the steamship *Gagara*, now renamed the *Kajak* by the Esthonian Government. From the affidavits filed on behalf of the plaintiffs, they had purchased the *Gagara* in 1914, registered the steamship and themselves as operators and owners the same year at Petrograd, Russia (now Leningrad), and they stated that the *Gagara* had flown the flag of the Russian Merchant Marine. During the early years of World War I the *Gagara* had been requisitioned in the service of the Czar's Imperial Government (Nicholas II) and that government and the steamship company had established mutually satisfactory relations and arrangements. Following the Russian Revolutions of 1917, the Bolshevik Government under Lenin's leadership came into power in Russia. On June 21, 1918, the Bolshevik Government declared by edict the whole of the Russian Merchant Marine to be national property and order the *Gagara*, then lying at anchor at Petrograd, to be repaired and returned to maritime service. The Bolshevik Government in the Fall of 1918

39

loaded the *Gagara* with a cargo of wood and sent the vessel on a routine business voyage to Copenhagen, Denmark. The ship's master was the original master who had been appointed by the steamship company some years earlier, and the majority of the ship's crew had been previously established crew members prior to the Russian Revolution. In the course of this voyage across the Baltic Sea to Copenhagen, Denmark, the *Gagara* put into the port of Reval, Esthonia, where the ship was interned and captured as a prize of war by the Esthonians.

As a result of this seizure by the Esthonian Government, affidavits were also filed by the Esthonian Government with the lower Admiralty Court stating their claims to ownership and control of the steamship *Gagara*, now *Kajak*. They stated that the *Gagara*, when making her appearance in the harbour at Reval, Esthonia, was flying the red flag of the Bolshevik Government, and she was accordingly condemned as a prize of war (Reds vs. Whites and Treaty of Brest-Litovsk) by a decree of the Esthonian Government. The *Gagara* was not brought before a Prize Court, but merely condemned as a prize of war by this governmental decree, eventually, she was renamed the *Kajak*, registered at Reval, Esthonia, as property of the Esthonian government, and she began to fly the Esthonian flag. Esthonia appointed a new master and a new crew for the *Kajak*. The cargo was now forwarded under the directions of the Esthonian Government and the Esthonian flag by the newly-appointed master to the port of London, England, where at that destination the cargo was to be transferred by a bill of lading to the representative of the Esthonian Government in London at that time. The *Kajak* arrived in London late in December 1918.

Meanwhile, back at Reval, Esthonia, the plaintiffs, on December 14, 1918, from their branch office in Reval, had forwarded a protest to the Esthonian Government against the seizure by them of the *Gagara*.

The protest was ignored by the Esthonian Government, and the plaintiffs then initiated action in England to recover the vessel. In London the managing director of the steamship company (plaintiffs), who was empowered to act for the company by holding the company's power of attorney, then secured the writ *in rem* to be served in London, and the subject of the proceedings then developed when the *Kajak* docked in London in late December.

On January 20, 1919, a motion was presented and made by the defendants to set aside the writ and the subsequent proceedings. The judges of the Admiralty Court then sought aid from the British

Foreign office to ascertain what they thought was the status of the Esthonian Government and State in relation to Britain. The Foreign Office on January 27, 1919, by verifiable correspondence indicated to the Admiralty Court that Esthonia was being recognized on the basis of a *de facto* independent body. Further, the Foreign Office indicated that the view of His Majesty's Government (George V), without in any way binding itself as to the future, felt the Esthonian Government was fully capable of setting up a Prize Court to enable them to handle such cases as the *Gagara* presented.

Accordingly, the Court of Appeal upheld the lower Admiralty Court and dismissed the appeal of the plaintiffs.

THE VINCENTI AFFAIR, 1920

Charles Vincenti, an American citizen, a known smuggler and rum-runner, was arrested by a special officer of the Department of Justice. Also, aiding this special officer in arresting Vincenti were two internal revenue agents. These three federal officers were collectively holding and enforcing a warrant against Vincenti for the unlawful sale of liquor in the state of Maryland. The three arresting officers made the arrest of Vincenti on board an American motorboat which at that time was located in British territorial waters off the island of Bimini, Bahama Islands, British West Indies.

Vincenti, it appeared from facts brought forth by U. S. mainland interrogation, had been induced or enjoined to board the American vessel by the three federal officers making the arrest. Subsequently, the American motorboat with Vincenti aboard had been challenged, pursued, and fired upon by British officials. However the American motorboat managed to out-run its British pursuers and returned Vincenti to the U. S. mainland for prosecution and trial.

The British government strongly protested the arrest and the violation of British jurisdiction in the territorial waters of the Bahama Islands.

Subsequently, the Department of State informed the British Ambassador that—"you will observe that the persons who arrested Charles Vincenti and forcibly removed him from the Bimini Islands, Bahamas, acted on their own initiative and without the knowledge or approval of this Government (U.S.A.) in any way, and have been reprimanded and indefinitely suspended for their participation in the affair. Furthermore, it appears that Vincenti's bail has been exonerated and all proceedings subsequent to his unlawful arrest have been revoked. The incident is greatly regretted by this Government, and I trust that the steps taken to make amends for it are entirely satisfactory to the British Government."

The British Ambassador replied that the action taken by the U. S. Government was satisfactory and acceptable to Britain.

WULFSOHN v. RUSSIAN SOCIALIST FEDERATED SOVIET REPUBLIC, 1923

United States, Court of Appeals of New York

This case emerged from an appeal by permission from an order issued by the Appellate Division of the Supreme Court, which had affirmed an order of Special Term denying a motion by the defendant (the U.S.S.R.) to vacate a warrant of attachment on that government by lower courts in New York. The lower courts in New York had decided that the Russian state was to be recognized but that its government was not and that the Bolshevik government could be sued, as any ordinary individual might be, and that the Russian government did not enjoy the immunities and privileges accorded a *de facto* or *de jure* status as a recognized government. The Appellate Division of the Supreme Court upheld the attachment awarded the plaintiff, Wulfsohn, and permitted an appeal by the defendant to be brought to the United States Court of Appeals of New York.

In recounting the facts, the plaintiff and his partners owned a large quantity of valuable furs which they had stored in warehouses in Russia. The Bolshevik Government, which assumed power in Russia after the Russian Revolutions of 1917, arbitrarily confiscated the furs held in storage in Russia and which were owned by the plaintiff, Wulfsohn, and his partners. The plaintiff then construed and treated this act as a conversion (unlawful seizure), and the aforementioned action was initiated. The litigation, then, did not involve equity with regard to title to property situated within the jurisdiction of our United States courts, where the end result depends upon the effect to be given to the action of a foreign government or where a decision or agreement could be reached through comity of the nations involved. This case presented a different problem for the courts to judge. The Bolshevik Government of Russia was sued by the plaintiff for an exercise of its sovereignty within its own geographic boundaries on the theory that such an act, if committed here in the United States by an individual or a group of individuals, would be a tort (willful injury to a plaintiff's person, property, or reputation) under the United States system of municipal law.

43

The plaintiff stated that, because of the non-recognition by the United States of the Bolshevik Government, such an action could be pursued and ultimately maintained. The United States Court of Appeals indicated that, while non-recognition and recognition was a problem area in the present case, there were more problem areas which existed and were also basic to the case and its end result. The court argued that, whether or not a government exists is determined by its ability and power to exert its authority in its contiguous geographic territory, by the manner in which the people it controls or rules obey, by the capability with which that government performs its duties and fulfills its obligations as an independent sovereign entity, and by the ability it may have in enforcing its claims by military force. These were the basic facts or criteria for evaluating whether or not a government exists and is recognized, and not upon a theoretical or hypothetical premise of recognition or non-recognition. Recognition does not create the state or government alone, although this may seem to be desirable in some instances.

In this case then, the court further stated that no proof of government existence is required. The fact is irrefutable, the Bolshevik Government exists and is sovereign within its boundaries and its jurisdiction in that territory is exclusive and absolute. Independence makes that government susceptible to no limitation or control except that which may be imposed by itself upon itself. The court then conceded that its (U.S.S.R.) actions should accord with natural justice and equity, but even if that government does not, our United States courts are not competent to review their performance. Our courts may not bring a foreign sovereign before them, not because of comity, but because that individual has not submitted himself to our legal system. Unless the foreign sovereign submits or consents to be subject to our laws, he is not subject to them, and the same holds true for a foreign government that has been accorded or recognized on a *de facto* or *de jure* basis. Thus, the government of the U.S.S.R. (Bolshevik) does exist and fulfills the requirements of a *de facto* nature, and we must recognize this fact of existence.

The court continued by stating that, whether a government was recognized or not, the detrimental results of the attempt and award made by our lower courts, even if morally and legally valid in our society, would strain international peace, disrupt the law of nations (International Law), and create crises and problems for our State Department which could not be resolved or adjudicated. The court indicated that the proper method of redress for a citizen of the

United States who has been wronged or suffered an injustice, such as the plaintiff's, is not through our system of courts, but to seek aid from our State Department, since the question or problem is international and political in nature. When an act, such as the U.S.S.R. enforced in this present case, is done by a sovereign state in its sovereign character, the only redress possible is through negotiation, reprisals, or resort to war.

Accordingly, the warrant of attachment and lower court orders are reversed by this court and the defendant's (U.S.S.R.) motion to vacate (free from) the warrant of attachment and lower court orders is upheld.

THE LUSITANIA CASES, 1923

United States - Germany, Mixed Claims Commission

On May 7, 1915, off the south coast of Ireland, the British luxury liner, *Lusitania*, was torpedoed and sunk by a German submarine without warning. This unwarranted sinking came during the period of American neutrality as World War I unfolded. At the time of the sinking, there were 197 American citizens aboard the *Lusitania*; of this group, 128 lost their lives and 69 were saved. The government of the 2nd Reich assumed liability for the losses and damages sustained by American citizens through its note of February 4, 1916, to the United States. The above cases were presented to the Mixed Claims Commission by the United States for consideration and reconciliation, and the determination of a formula for determining the estimates for said losses and damages as a result of the sinking of the *Lusitania* on May 7, 1915.

The Commission finds that Germany is financially obligated to pay to the United States all losses suffered by American nationals, stated in terms of dollars, where the claims therefore have continued in American ownership, which losses have resulted from death or from personal injury or from loss of, or damage to, property sustained in the sinking of the *Lusitania*.

This finding disposes of this group of claims, save that there remain to be considered (1) issues involving the nationality of each claimant affecting the Commission's jurisdiction and (2) the measure of damages to be applied to the facts of each case.

In this decision rules applicable to the measure of damages in death cases will be considered. In formulating such rules and determining the weight to be given to the decisions of court and tribunals dealing with this subject, it is important to bear in mind the basis of recovery in death cases in the jurisdictions announcing such decisions.

At common law there existed no cause of action for damages caused by death of a human being. The right to maintain such actions has, however, been long conferred by statutes enacted by Great Britain and by. all of the American States. The German Code expressly recognizes liability for the taking of life. These legislative enactments vary in their terms to such an extent that there cannot be evolved from them and the decisions of the courts construing them any composite uniform rules governing this branch of the law. Such statutes and decisions, as well as the other governing principles set out in this Commission's Administrative Decision No. 2, will, however, be considered in determining the applicable rules governing the measuring of damages in death cases.

The statutes enacted in common-law jurisdictions conferring a cause of action in death cases where none before existed have frequently limited by restrictive terms the rules for measuring damages in such cases. The tendency, however, of both statutes and decisions is to give such elasticity to these restrictive rules as to enable courts and juries in applying them to the facts of each particular case to award full and fair compensation for the injury suffered and the loss sustained. The statutes of several States of the American Union authorize juries to award such damages as are "fair and just" or "proportionate to the injury." Under such statutes the decisions of the courts give to the juries much broader latitude in assessing damages than those of other States where the statutes expressly limit them to so-called "pecuniary injuries", which is a term much misunderstood.

In most of the jurisdictions where civil law is administered and where the right of action for injuries resulting in death has long existed independent of any code or statute containing restrictions on rules for measuring damages, the courts have not been hampered in so formulating such rules and adapting them to the facts of each case as to give complete compensation for the loss sustained.

It is a general rule of both the civil and the common law that every invasion of private right imports an injury and that for every such injury the law gives a remedy. Speaking generally, that remedy must be commensurate with the injury received. It is variously expressed as "compensation", "reparation", "indemnity", "recompense", and is measured by pecuniary standards, because, says Grotius, "money is the common measure of valuable things".

In death cases the right of action is for the loss sustained by the claimants, not by the estate. The basis of damages is, not the physical or mental sufferings of deceased or his loss or the loss to his estate, but the losses resulting to claimants from his death. The enquiry then is: What amount will compensate claimants for such losses?

Bearing in mind that we are not concerned with any problems involving the punishment of a wrongdoer but only with the naked question of fixing the amount which will compensate for the wrong done, our formula expressed in general terms for reaching that end is: Estimate the amounts (1) which the decedent, had he not been killed, would probably have contributed to the claimant, add thereto (b) the pecuniary value to such claimant of the deceased's personal services in claimant's care, education, or supervision, and also add (c) reasonable compensation for such mental suffering or shock, if any, caused by the violent severing of family ties, as claimant may actually have sustained by reason of such death. The sum of these estimates, reduced to its present cash value, will generally represent the loss sustained by claimant.

In making such estimates there will be considered, among other factors, the following:

(a) The age, sex, health, condition and station in life, occupation, habits of industry and sobriety, mental and physical capacity, frugality, earning capacity and customary earnings of the deceased and the uses made of such earnings by him;

(b) The probable direction of the life of deceased but for the fatal injury, in arriving at which standard life-expectancy tables and all other pertinent evidence offered will be considered;

(c) The reasonable probability that the earning capacity of deceased, had he lived, would either have increased or decreased;

(d) The age, sex, health, condition and station in life, and probable expectancy of each of the claimants;

(e) The extent to which the deceased, had he lived, would have applied his income from his earnings or otherwise to his personal expenditures from which claimants would have derived no benefits;

(f) In reducing to their present cash value contributions which would probably have been made from time to time to claimants by deceased, a 5% interest rate and standard present-value tables will be used;

(g) Neither the physical pain nor the mental anguish which the deceased may have suffered will be considered as elements of damage;

(h) The amount of insurance on the life of the deceased collected by his estate or by the claimants will not be taken into account in computing the damages which claimants may be entitled to recover;

(i) No exemplary, punitive, or vindictive damages can be assessed.

Evaluate these criteria for assessing claims; are they adequate or inadequate? How would you arrive at establishing criteria for claims of this type, and what would your criteria for evaluation be? What is your candid opinion of the 2nd Reich's use of the U-Boat as a revolutionary weapon and the sinking of the *Lusitania*? Are there any similarities between the *Lusitania* sinking in World War I and the Hiroshima and Nagasaki bombings of World War II? Differences? How does the response of the 2nd Reich concerning moral responsibility for the *Lusitania* differ from the American response for moral responsibility at Hiroshima and Nagasaki in World War II? What are the "pros and cons" in comparing these tragedies? Enumerate!

SOKOLOFF v. NATIONAL CITY BANK, 1924

United States, Court of Appeals of New York

This case was heard by this court upon the initiation of an appeal, by permission, from an order by the Appellate Division of the Supreme Court to permit all aspects of this case to come under judicial scrutiny and interpretation. The Court of Appeals then heard the case upon the pleadings presented.

The background facts are· as follows: In June of 1917, Sokoloff (plaintiff) paid to the National City Bank (defendant) in New York City $30,225. The bank then promised Sokoloff that they would open an account for him in their branch bank at Petrograd (now Leningrad) in Imperial Russia. The bank further stated that they would repay Sokoloff the sum which he had deposited in New York City, $30,225, at the rate of 23¼ cents per ruble, or a total of 130,000 rubles. Sokoloff could, at such times and in such amounts as he deemed necessary, write demands or orders on this branch bank account at Petrograd until he had completely withdrawn or closed said account.

Sokoloff, after stating what the agreement had been between himself and the bank, said that the account had been opened in Petrograd by the branch bank and that he had, from time to time, withdrawn against the opening balance of 130,000 rubles, until in November 1917 a balance of 128,000 rubles or $28,365 remained. In the following months, Sokoloff had presented written orders for honoring and payment; these written orders were dishonored and non-payment by the branch bank followed. Sokoloff, the plaintiff, then filed suit for recovery of his 128,000 rubles ($28,365) from the National City Bank, the defendant.

The defendant (National City Bank) based its defense upon two questions which the Court of Appeals certified and directed their answer in arriving at a decision in the case.

The first defense and question evolved from the after-effects of the Bolshevik Revolution of 1917; the Bolshevik assumption of power, its nationalization of the banking industry in Russia, the use of forced arms to accomplish this fact, and the ultimate establishment of a State Bank under Bolshevik control. The defendant argued that, as a result of the Bolshevik Revolution of 1917, the new Bolshevik government became liable for the defendant's debt by its decreed nationalization edict, its confiscation of all Russian bank assets, and the crediting of these assets to the account of a revolutionary tax. Furthermore, the defendant stated by an averment (positive statement) that the plaintiff (Sokoloff) was fully aware of the probability of future political and governmental changes; that the agreement between the plaintiff and the defendant should be performed and consummated in Russia; therefore, the laws of Russia should govern the agreement and performance of it; and, should any orders or decrees be enacted, the government in Russia would be the basic authority. By reason of these facts, the plaintiff's deposit account is said to have been seized, his title thereto divested, and the defendant's liability discharged.

The second defense is the same as the first, except that it pleads the facts as a partial defense, rather than a complete one, and introduces the question of recognition and non-recognition of the U.S.S.R. The Court of Appeals argued that the Russian Government was not here in court either as a plaintiff or as a defendant. A domestic corporation pleads the acts and mandates of that government to excuse a default and discharge an obligation. The question of recognition and non-recognition by the United States is not a final factor in this case, but the basis for the cases rests upon the performance and obligation attendant with an executory contract. This contract the defendant has not performed, and the defendant refuses to return the dollars that were paid by the plaintiff upon the promise of performance. The defendant's liability was unaffected by the attempt to terminate its existence and seizure of its assets by the Russian Government.

The Court of Appeals decided that restitution remained due, holding that recognition was controlling and that effect should not be given to the decrees of an unrecognized government. The Court affirmed the order and restitution was made mandatory.

UNITED STATES (NORTH AMERICAN DREDGING CO. CLAIM) v. UNITED MEXICAN STATES, 1926

United States - Mexico, General Claims Commission

This claim was put forward by the United States of America on behalf of the North American Dredging Company of Texas, an American corporation. The North American Dredging Company asked for recovery of the sum of $233,523.30 with interest to be added to the recovery sum claimed for losses and damages alleged to have been sustained by the dredging company for breaches of contract which arose as a result of non-performance of contractual obligations by the Mexican government. The contract had been entered into between the dredging company and the Mexican government on November 23, 1912, for dredging the port of Salina Cruz, Mexico. This contract had been signed at Mexico City, and the government of Mexico had been a party to the contract. Both signatories had entered this contract in good faith and obligation. The services and subject matter of the contract—for example, the dredging company's services to be rendered and the Mexican government's method of paying for these services performed—were enumerated in the contract. Also, payment was to be made in Mexico. The conflicting issue over which this claim arose and was set in motion was Article 18 of the contract subject matter which the Mexican government incorporated as an indispensable provision, not separable from other provisions of said contract; and the dredging company agreed to Article 18 since the contract could not be secured without compliance to Article 18. The controversial Article 18 reads as follows:

The contractor and all persons, who, as employees or in any other capacity may be engaged in the execution of work under this contract either directly or indirectly, shall be considered as Mexicans in all matters, within the Republic of Mexico, concerning the execution of such work, and the fulfillment of this contract. They shall not claim, nor shall they have, with regard to the interests and the business connected with this contract, any other rights or means to enforce the same than those granted by the laws of the Republic to Mexicans, nor shall they enjoy any other rights than those established in favor of Mexicans. They are consequently deprived of any rights as aliens, and under no conditions shall the intervention of foreign diplomatic agents be permitted, in any matter related to this contract. (NOTE* Basis is Calvo clause and doctrine.)

The Mexican agent then asked the General Claims Commission to dismiss the claim of the North American Dredging Company.

The basis upon which the Mexican agent asked for dismissal of the claim by the dredging company was predicated upon two factors: first, the Mexican agent stated that claims based on alleged non-performance of contract obligations were outside the jurisdiction of the Commission; and, second, that a contract which contained the so-called Calvo clause deprives the party subscribing to that clause of the right to submit any claims connected with his contract to international scrutiny and adjudication.

The Commission decided that the case as presented is not within its jurisdiction and the motion of the Mexican agent to dismiss the claim is sustained. The case was thereby dismissed without prejudice to the claimant to pursue his remedies elsewhere or to seek remedies before this commission for claims arising after the signing of the Treaty between the United States and Mexico of September 8, 1923.

NOTE: The Calvo Doctrine

In his treatise on International Law concerning its theory and practice, published in 1896, Carlos Calvo, a famous Argentinian jurist, maintained the notion of non-responsibility of States for losses of aliens resulting from a civil war or an insurrection as a general principle. He stated that, were the new governments or states to admit responsibility, they would establish an unjustifiable inequality between the new nationals and the aliens or foreigners. Primarily, what the Calvo Doctrine provided the newly-emerging Latin American states with, in legal parlance, was the use by a foreigner of local remedies to seek redress by law and to insulate these new states from foreign intervention and extraterritoriality.

NOTE:

In a rehearing of this case in 1947 by an American-Mexican Claims Commission established by an Act of Congress in 1942 and the Mexican state, the Calvo Doctrine was declared invalid and the Commission awarded the dredging company the sum of $128,627.77 with interest.

UNITED STATES (JANES CLAIM) v. MEXICO, 1926

United States - Mexico, General Claims Commission

This claim was made by the United States of America against Mexico for damages and losses amounting to $25,000 which were suffered on the account of the murder of Byron E. Janes, an American citizen, on July 10, 1918, at the El Tigre Mining Company, El Tigre, Sonora, Mexico. The United States presented the claim against Mexico on behalf of Jane's widow, Laura, their two children Byron, Jr., and Addison, and immediate family, Elizabeth and Catherine Janes.

Six months preceding the fatal tragedy, Mr. Byron Janes had been installed as Mine Superintendent of the El Tigre Mine Company. During this early period Superintendent Janes had had a good deal of trouble with a trammer (miner) named Pedro Carbajal; subsequently, Janes had given orders for his discharge.

The employment office for the El Tigre Mining Company was the main office for the company, located near the entrance to the #4 mine shaft, and about 100 yards from the American quarters in the town of El Tigre itself. Several evenings prior to the tragedy, Carbajal had visited the employment office at the main mine office, requesting that he be rehired and reinstated in his former position as a miner; Carbajal was refused in his new application. On July 10, 1918, at about 3:30 P.M., Carbajal again entered the employment office seeking to be re-employed, and was again refused.

Shortly thereafter, both Superintendent Janes and Mr. W. Williams, an employee of the El Tigre Mining Company, left the main mine office and began making their way across the intervening space between the main office and the American quarters. When both men were about half way across the intervening space, Carbajal came rushing after them, brandishing a revolver in the air. Both Americans heard him approaching; Superintendent Janes turned, dodged by Carbajal, and ran towards the main mine office; Williams stood still and said "don't shoot". Carbajal aimed point blank at Williams, but his revolver failed to fire. He then turned and squeezed off a shot at Janes, who was running for cover; he hit him in the middle of the back, dropping Janes immediately. Carbajal then ran up to the wounded and fallen Janes and put a second shot through his brain, killing Janes outright.

Carbajal then frightened off bystanders and onlookers with his revolver and fled up a nearby canyon to escape apprehension.

The Police Commissioner was advised of the cold-blooded murder some five minutes later. It took him and his men almost half an hour to prepare a posse for the pursuit of Carbajal. The El Tigre Mining Company supplied them with horses to aid in the search. At about 7:00 P.M. the Police Commissioner and his posse returned to El Tigre and reported no success in finding or locating the whereabouts of Carbajal. On the following day the Police Commissioner and his posse again scoured the countryside without success.

Local people later stated that Carbajal had stayed at a ranch some 6 miles south of El Tigre for a week and had even returned to the local bistro on several occasions during that ensuing week to flaunt the law and partake of liquid refreshment.

Later, word was received that Carbajal was working at a mescal (liquor plant) near Carrizal, some 75 miles south of El Tigre. The proper civil and military authorities in the area were made aware of this fact, and the Mining Company offered a large reward for Carbajal's capture, but when the authorities arrived at the mescal plant in Carrizal, Carbajal had fled and was not apprehended, nor has been since that time.

From the aforementioned events and facts, the present claim by the United States against Mexico was presented on behalf of Janes' survivors. The Commission decided that the Mexican Government is obligated to pay to the United States Government $12,000 (twelve thousand dollars), without interest, on behalf of Janes' survivors. The Mexican Government and local authorities were adjudged to have been delinquent in their pursuit of justice and maintenance of law and order.

UNITED STATES (NEER CLAIM) v. MEXICO, 1926

United States - Mexico, General Claims Commission

The United States presented this claim against Mexico for $100,000 on behalf of the widow, Fay L. Neer, and her daughter, Pauline, as a result of the murder of her husband, Paul Neer, by a person or persons unknown, on November 16, 1924, at about 8:00 P.M. in the evening as Mr. and Mrs. Neer were proceeding from the village of Guanacevi, Durango, Mexico, to their home nearby. At the time of his death, Paul Neer was employed as superintendent of a mine in the immediate vicinity of Guanacevi, State of Durango, Mexico.

The events unfolded as follows: As Mr. and Mrs. Neer were riding on horseback from the village of Guanacevi to their home in the immediate area at about 8:00 P.M. in the evening, they were hailed and halted by a band of armed men also on horseback, who proceeded to engage Mr. Neer in conversation. As Mrs. Neer did not understand what was being said, she was not able to explain later why the conversation broke up and a terrific exchange of gunfire took place between her husband and the armed men. It was during this frantic exchange of gunfire between Neer and the armed group that Neer fell mortally wounded and died almost immediately. Mrs. Neer quickly informed the local Police Commissioner, and he in turn set the wheels of justice in motion the following day. Mrs. Neer—the only eyewitness to the murder—was not able to provide much in the way of leads for the local authorities to pursue. Both the Mexican civil and military authorities were active in attempting to solve this murder; and, after considerable investigation, several arrests were made of suspects, who were subsequently released due to lack of evidence.

It is thus alleged by the United States on behalf of Neer's widow and daughter that, due to this unwarranted murder, they have sustained damages and losses amounting to $100,000 and, if the Mexican authorities had exercised diligent and intelligent investigation, the culprits could have been apprehended and justice done. Therefore, the United States presented the Neer claim to the Mexican government that the claimants ought to be paid the stated amount.

In this particular case, the Commission held that the Mexican Government and local authorities were not delinquent in their investigation and the diligence with which the investigation was pursued. The Commission indicated that the Mexican Government and local authorities had conducted an intelligent investigation and pursued it with complete records, vigor, and diligence.

The Commission then decided that the claim of the United States is disallowed.

DICKINSON v. Del SOLAR, 1929

Great Britain, King's Bench Division

This action was instituted against Emilio Del Solar by Robert E. Dickinson, who sought to recover damages and losses for injuries received as a result of Mr. Del Solar's negligence and careless driving of his car and resulting injuries sustained by Mr. Dickinson. The jury and court awarded Mr. Dickinson damages to the amount of $4,500 (L. 856), and Mr. Del Solar, in addition, had to pay the court costs.

However, the case took a new turn when Mr. Del Solar indicated that he had a liability insurance coverage policy with the Mobile and General Insurance Company, Ltd., London, England, and that he, Mr. Del Solar, should be indemnified and recompensed by the insurance company for the damages awarded by the court to the plaintiff, Dickinson.

In turn, the insurance company argued that Mr. Del Solar, who was the First Secretary of the Peruvian Legation, was clothed with diplomatic immunity and therefore immune from the civil law process in Great Britain and that the court did not have jurisdiction in this case. Due to these new circumstances, the insurance company argued for recognition of diplomatic immunity for Mr. Del Solar, which would free him and the insurance company from all obligations to Mr. Dickinson and make the damages awarded null and void.

Mr. Del Solar enjoined proceedings to transfer his obligations to the insurance company, so that his insurance coverage and subsequent claim would be paid by the insurance company and he would still be clothed with protection by them in the future.

It was at this point that the Minister of the Peruvian Legation intervened and gave direction to a decision by forbidding Mr. Del Solar to rely upon diplomatic immunity. The Minister of the Peruvian Legation stated that the collision had occurred when the car was being used, not for the official business of the Peruvian Legation, but for private purposes. Finally, a letter was written on March 5, 1929, by Mr. Del Solar's lawyers to the attorneys representing the insurance company. It read as follows:

We have seen His Excellency the Peruvian Minister personally on this matter and he has definitely repeated the instructions he has already given to his first secretary, Mr. Del Solar, to the effect that diplomatic privilege is not to be pleaded in this action; in our submission, therefore, the effect is that, so far at any rate as this claim is concerned, Mr. Del Solar has not and never did have any diplomatic privilege at all, so that it is impossible for him to claim it even if he wished to do so.

The court concluded that diplomatic agents are not, in recognition of their immunities and privileges as such, immune from legal liability for any wrongful acts. To be accurate, the Court continued, is that they are not liable to be sued in the English Courts unless they submit to jurisdiction. Diplomatic privilege does not import immunity from legal liability, but only exemption from local jurisdiction. In the present case the privilege was waived and jurisdiction was submitted to by the entry of Mr. Del Solar.

The Court, therefore, held that the third party (the insurance company) was liable for the damages and costs.

UNITED STATES v. FLORES, 1933

United States Supreme Court

Santos Flores, an American citizen, murdered a fellow shipmate and American citizen during an argument on board the S. S. *Padnsay*, an American vessel employed in overseas trade. This deed occurred while the *Padnsay* was at anchor at the port of Matadi in the former Belgian Congo, now the Republic of the Congo. The port of Matadi is located some 250 miles inland from the mouth of the Congo River and the Atlantic Ocean and is the major port for the Congo area. The *Padnsay* was anchored and attached to the shore at the port of Matadi by cables; at the time of the murder the vessel was being unloaded of her cargo. The port of Matadi and the Belgian Congo were at the time of the murder under the jurisdiction and sovereignty of the Kingdom of Belgium.

Following the murder, Flores was returned in custody aboard the S. S. *Padnsay* to the Port of Philadelphia and within the jurisdiction of the District Court of that area, where he was indicted for murder. The District Court of Philadelphia sustained a demurrer (hesitant action) to the indictment and discharged the prisoner on the ground that the court was without jurisdiction to try the offense charged.

The United States appealed the decision of the Pennsylvania District Court to the United States Supreme Court, where the case was again heard and a decision reached concerning Santos Flores and U. S. jurisdiction in the case.

The Supreme Court argued that it is true that the criminal jurisdiction of the United States is in general based on the territorial principle, and criminal laws or statutes of the United States are not by implication to be given extraterritorial effect. However, the Court continued that this principle has never been thought to be applicable to a merchant vessel which, for purposes of the jurisdiction of the courts of the sovereignty whose flag it flies to punish crimes committed aboard it, is construed to be a part of the territory of that sovereign entity, and it will not lose that character when in navigable waters within the territorial jurisdiction and sovereignty of another state. Concurrent jurisdiction may be indicated in some instances, but in the vast majority of cases in the maritime field, unless the tranquillity or peace of the foreign sovereign state is disturbed, jurisdiction will be retained by the flag the vessel flies and the sovereign state it represents. Thus, in view of the wide recognition of the principle of extraterritorial jurisdiction over crimes committed on merchant vessels and its customary and statutory acceptance by the United States and other western nation-states, the United States does have jurisdiction in this case.

In the absence of any controlling treaty provision and any assertion of jurisdiction by the territorial sovereign state, Belgium, it is the duty of the United States to apply its own laws to offenses committed by its own citizens on vessels flying the U. S. flag and interpret them in the light of recognized principles of International Law. The United States has jurisdiction in this case. Consequently, the indictment must be sustained and the judgment and demurrer of the lower court must be reversed.

THE I'M ALONE, 1933

United States - Canada, Claims Commission

The notorious Canadian liquor smuggling schooner, *I'm Alone*, was hailed on March 20, 1929, by the United States Coast Guard cutter *Wolcott* off the bayou coast of Louisiana in the Gulf of Mexico. The *I'm Alone* was outside the three-mile jurisdiction limit when sighted and hailed, but she was less than one hour's sailing time in distance from the Louisiana shoreline. The master of the *I'm Alone*, upon being hailed, refused to stop and permit the request of the U. S. Coast Guard cutter *Wolcott* to search the *I'm Alone*. The *I'm Alone* then unfurled all sails and applied all power possible in heading for the open sea with the cutter in hot pursuit. Three blank shots were fired by the cutter *Wolcott* across the bow of the notorious *I'm Alone*. These shots were disregarded by the skipper of the *I'm Alone*, and under her master's orders she continued her pell-mell rush toward the open waters of the Gulf of Mexico. The cutter *Wolcott* then proceeded to fire live shells through the sails and rigging of the *I'm Alone* in order to bring her to heave to and permit the *Wolcott* to search her. Unfortunately, the deck gun on the *Wolcott* jammed at this juncture, but she continued the hot pursuit of the *I'm Alone*.

The *Wolcott* then radioed that another revenue cutter be sent to aid her in the chase, which continued all during the ensuing days of March 21 and 22 when both the *I'm Along* and *Wolcott* were several hundreds of miles south of the Louisiana coast in the Gulf of Mexico. During the day of March 22 the *Wolcott* was joined by the U. S. Coast Guard cutter *Dexter*. The *I'm Alone* was again warned to heave to; the master of the *I'm Alone* again ignored this warning from the Coast Guard cutters; and the cutter *Dexter* then proceeded to sink the *I'm Alone*.

The master and crew of the latter, with the exception of the boatswain, Leon Mainguy, who drowned, were rescued from the high seas by the U. S. cutters and returned to the U. S. mainland for interrogation and remedial procedures.

The Canadian Government contended in its claim before the *ad hoc* Commission, convened and staffed under the provisions of Article IV of the Convention of January 23, 1924, between the United States and Canada for the suppression of the smuggling of intoxicating liquors into the United States, *inter alia* (among things), that the doctrine of hot pursuit "has not found complete acceptance" and "where recognized, it is under the distinct limitation that the pursuit is not hot or continuous when another vessel is substituted for the original pursuing vessel; nor does the doctrine permit the sinking of the vessel pursued; nor is the doctrine recognized where pursuit has been initiated outside territorial waters".

The American Government replied that our Federal Courts had applied the doctrine of hot pursuit to the "seizure on the high seas of vessels suspected of violating the laws of the United States, not from our territorial waters, but from the distance of one hour's sailing time from the coast of the United States". Furthermore, the United States Government stated that the *Wolcott* was present from the start of pursuit to the sinking of the *I'm Alone*; the master of the *I'm Alone* preferred to be sunk than be taken into custody and court for adjudication; no crew members were injured by the gun fire; and, if sufficient life preservers had been on board the *I'm Alone*, the life of Mr. Leon Mainguy would have been spared.

Further evidence was introduced by the United States to the effect that, although the *I'm Alone* was registered as a Canadian vessel, the beneficial ownership of the vessel was American.

The Commissioners consider that, in view of the facts, no compensation ought to be paid in respect of the loss of the ship or the cargo.

The act of sinking the ship, however, by officers of the United States Coast Guard, was, as we have already indicated, an unlawful act; and the Commissioners consider that the United States ought formally to acknowledge its illegality, and to apologize to His Majesty's Canadian Government therefor; and, further, that as a material amend in respect of the wrong the United States should pay the sum of $25,000 to His Majesty's Canadian Government; and they recommend accordingly.

The Commissioners have had under consideration the compensation which ought to be paid by the United States to His Majesty's Canadian Government for the benefit of the captain and members of the crew, none of whom was a party to the illegal conspiracy to smuggle liquor into the United States and sell the same there. (An additional sum of $25,666.50 was thereupon recommended for the benefit of the captain and crew.)

CHUNG CHI CHEUNG v. THE KING, 1938

Great Britain, Judicial Committee of the Privy Council

This is an appeal to the Judicial Committee of the Privy Council entertained by Chung Chi to have his conviction and sentence by trial and jury by the Supreme Court of Hong Kong, and the subsequent dismissal of his appeal by judgment of the Full Court of Hong Kong again reviewed and adjudicated.

Chung Chi, the appellant, had been convicted of the murder of the captain of the vessel, *Cheung Keng*, Douglas L. Campbell, and sentenced to death. The murder of Captain Campbell had been committed by Chung Chi, a cabin boy, on board the Chinese Maritime Customs Cruiser, *Cheung Keng*, while that vessel was in Hong Kong territorial waters. Both Captain Campbell and Chung Chi were in the service of the Chinese Government on board the cruiser at the time of the murder. Both the captain and the cabin boy were British nationals. The point of contention from which the present appeal emerged was the fact that the murder had taken place on an armed public vessel of the foreign Chinese government, and Chung Chi contended that the British Court had no jurisdiction in the matter. The Chief Justice of the Hong Kong Supreme Court overruled this contention and said they had jurisdiction. On the subsequent appeal, the Full Court of Hong Kong upheld the earlier decision that the Supreme Court had jurisdiction.

To clarify the legal position of the British, the basic material facts must be reconstructed: On January 11, 1937, Chung Chi shot and killed Captain Campbell on board the cruiser *Cheung Keng*. After committing this dastardly deed, Chung Chi continued on up the ladder to the bridge of the vessel where he shot at and wounded the acting chief officer. He then retired below deck and shot and wounded himself. The wounded acting chief officer then directed the boatswain to proceed to Hong Kong at full speed and hail the first police launch in sight, in order that the wounded acting chief officer could have the aid of the Hong Kong police in making the arrest of the accused. A short time later, when the launch of the Hong Kong water police came alongside in answer to the *Cheung Keng's* signal, both of the wounded men, the first officer and the prisoner, were removed and taken to the hospital in Hong Kong. The Hong Kong water police also took possession of two revolvers with which the accused had armed himself, the expended shells and spent revolver bullets, and some unexpended cartridges found with the accused.

The chairman of the Provincial Government of Kwangtang Nationalist China commenced extradition proceedings on February 25, 1938, to have the accused, Chung Chi, tried for alleged and attempted murder in that Chinese province, since the Chinese indicated that the crime had been committed on a Chinese Customs cruiser in Chinese waters.

It is upon this extradition attempt, and the question of jurisdiction, that the present appeal was carried to Great Britain by Chung Chi.

The Privy Council argued that on the question of jurisdiction two theories have found favor with persons who profess a knowledge of the principles of International Law. The first theory is that a public ship with national identity is, for all purposes, either a part of the territory of the nation to which she belongs or is to be treated by other nations on that basis, unless dire emergencies, acts, or events occur which necessitate concurrent jurisdiction or assumption of jurisdiction by the local territory or state. The second theory is that a public ship in foreign waters is not, and is not treated as, territory of her own nation. Based on related principles of International Law, the domestic courts will accord to the public ship, its crew, and its cargo certain immunities, some of which are well established and some which are in dispute. In this view the immunities do not depend on the concept of objective extraterritoriality, but on what the implications of the domestic law indicate. The implications are conditional in nature and may be waived by the nation to which the public ship belongs. In this case their Lordships entertain no doubt that the second theory is the correct conclusion and that the lower courts in Hong Kong had jurisdiction.

The Privy Council next asked themselves, What are the immunities of public ships of other nations under the jurisdiction of our courts, and on what principle are they based?

In the present case the question arises as to the murder of one ship's officer and the wounding and attempted murder of another ship's officer by a member of the crew of that ship. On these facts alone without greater implications, the Nationalist Chinese Government could clearly have had jurisdiction over the act because, even though Chung Chi had been taken to and cared for in a

Hong Kong hospital, a diplomatic request for his surrender to Chinese officials would have been in order. The fact that all parties involved in the tragedy were British nationals would not have altered the fact that they were all members of the crew of a Nationalist Chinese ship. No diplomatic request was ever presented or made. The only request by the Chinese Government was for extradition, which was based on treaty and statutory rights; and, because of the circumstances in this case, extradition was doomed to failure.

Consequently, in applying these considerations to this case, it appears that the Chinese Government, once the extradition proceedings were finalized, consented to British jurisdiction. Further evidence of Chinese compliance to British jurisdiction was indicated when on two different occasions they permitted four (4) members of their service to give evidence in the British courts and permitted the material instruments of conviction (revolver, bullets, etc.) to remain in the hands of the Hong Kong police without a demur (hesitant action).

It, therefore, follows that there was no valid objection to British jurisdiction and the appeal of Chung Chi Cheung fails.

For the above reasons their Lordships hereby advised his Majesty *(Rex)* to dismiss the appeal. Appeal dismissed and sentence and conviction upheld.

HINES v. DAVIDOWITZ, et. al.; 1941

United States Supreme Court

This case developed out of an appeal from a decree of a United States District Court in Pennsylvania consisting of three judges who issued the decree restraining (holding back) the authorities of the Commonwealth of Pennsylvania from enforcing against an alien (Davidowitz) specific provisions pertaining to the registration of aliens by the Pennsylvania Alien Registration Act of 1939 which had become a state statute as World War II began in Europe. The three federal judges decided that the Pennsylvania Alien Registration Act of 1939 denied aliens equal protection of the laws and that the Pennsylvania Act encroached upon the federal government's constitutionally vested legislative powers. In 1940 the Pennsylvania Act was held to be unconstitutional, and Congress enacted a federal Registration Act for Aliens on June 28, 1940, which was of a uniform nature for the then 48 states.

In recounting the historic background facts, two very important considerations are recognized: first, that the supremacy of the national power in the general field of foreign affairs, including power over immigration, naturalization and deportation, is made clear by the Constitution; this was pointed out by the authors of *The Federalist* in 1787 and has since been given continuous recognition by this Court. When the national government by treaty or statute has established rules and regulations touching the rights, privileges, obligations or burdens of aliens as such, the treaty or statute is the supreme law of the land. No state can add to or take from the force and effect of such treaty or statute, for Article VI of the Constitution provides that "This Constitution, and the Laws of the United States which shall be made in Pursuance thereof; and all Treaties made, or which shall be made, under the Authority of the United States, shall be the supreme Law of the Land; and the Judges in every State shall be bound thereby, any Thing in the Constitution or Laws of any State to the Contrary notwithstanding". The Federal Government, representing as it does the collective interests of the forty-eight states, is entrusted with full and exclusive responsibility for the conduct of affairs with foreign sovereignties. "For local interests the several states of the Union exist, but for national purposes, embracing our relations with foreign nations, we are but one people, one nation, one power". Our system of government is such that the interest of the cities, counties and states no less than the interest of the people of the whole nation, imperatively requires that federal power in the field affecting foreign relations be left entirely free from local interference. As Mr. Justice Miller observed of a California statute burdening immigration: "If (the United States) should get into a difficulty which would lead to war, or to suspension of intercourse, would California alone suffer, or all the Union?"

One of the most important and delicate of all international relationships, recognized immemorially as a responsibility of government, has to do with the protection of the just rights of a country's own nationals when those nationals are in another country. Experience has shown that international controversies of the gravest moment, sometimes even leading to war, may arise from real or imagined wrongs to another's subjects inflicted, or permitted, by a government. This country, like other nations, has entered into numerous treaties of amity and commerce since its inception—treaties entered into under express constitutional authority, and binding upon the states as well as the nation. Among those treaties have been many which not only promised and guaranteed broad rights and privileges to aliens sojourning in our own territory, but secured reciprocal promises and guarantees for our own citizens while in other lands. And apart from treaty obligations, there has grown up in the field of international relations a body of customs defining with more or less certainty the duties owing by all nations to alien residents—duties which our State Department has often successfully insisted foreign nations must recognize as to our nationals abroad. In general, both treaties and international practices have been aimed at preventing injurious discriminations against aliens. Concerning such treaties, this Court has said: "While treaties, in safeguarding important rights in the interest of reciprocal beneficial relations, may be their express terms afford a measure of protection to aliens which citizens of one or both of the parties may not be able to demand against their own government, the general purpose of treaties of amity and commerce is to avoid injurious discrimination in either country against the citizens of the other."

Legal imposition of distinct, unusual and extraordinary burdens and obligations upon aliens—such as subjecting them alone, though perfectly law-abiding, to indiscriminate and repeated interception and interrogation by public officials—thus bears an inseparable relationship to the welfare and tranquillity of all the states, and not merely to the welfare and tranquillity of one. Laws imposing such burdens are not mere census requirements, and even though they may be immediately associated with the accomplishment of a local purpose, they provoke questions in the field of international affairs. And specialized regulation of the conduct of an alien before naturalization is a matter which Congress must consider in discharging its constitutional duty "To establish an Uniform Rule of Naturalization...". It cannot be doubted that both the state and federal registration laws belong "to that class of laws which concern the exterior relation of this whole nation with other nations and governments." Consequently, the regulation of aliens is so intimately blended and intertwined with responsibilities of the national government that where it acts, and the state also acts on the same subject, "the act of Congress, or the treaty, is supreme; and the law of the State, though enacted in the exercise of powers not controverted, must yield to it." And where the federal government, in the exercise of its superior authority in this field, has enacted a complete scheme of regulation and has therein provided a standard for the registration of aliens, states cannot, inconsistently with the purpose of Congress, conflict or interfere with, curtail or complement the federal law, or enforce additional or auxiliary regulations. There is not—and from the very nature of the problem there cannot be—any rigid formula or rule which can be used as a universal pattern to determine the meaning and purpose of every act of Congress. This Court, in considering the validity of state laws in the light of treaties of federal laws touching the same subject, has made use of the following expressions: conflicting; contrary to; occupying the field; repugnance; difference; irreconcilability; inconsistency; violation; curtailment; and interference. But none of these expressions provides an infallible constitutional test or an exclusive constitutional yardstick. In the final analysis, there can be no one crystal clear distinctly marked formula. Our primary function is to determine whether, under the circumstances of this particular case, Pennsylvania's law stands as an obstacle to the accomplishment and execution of the full purposes and objectives of Congress. And in that determination, it is of importance that this legislation is in a field which affects international relations, the one aspect of our government that from the first has been most generally conceded imperatively to demand broad national authority. Any concurrent state power that may exist is restricted to the narrowest of limits; the state's power here is not bottomed on the same broad base as is its power to tax. And it is also of importance that this legislation deals with the rights, liberties, and personal freedoms of human beings, and is in an entirely different category from state tax statutes or state pure food laws regulating the labels on cans.

Our conclusion is that the appellee is correct in his contention that the power to restrict, limit, regulate, and register aliens as a distinct group is not an equal and continuously existing concurrent power of state and nation, but that whatever power a state may have is subordinate to supreme national law. We proceed, therefore, to an examination of Congressional enactments to ascertain whether or not Congress has acted in such a manner that its action should preclude enforcement of Pennsylvania's law.

For many years Congress has provided a broad and comprehensive plan describing the terms and conditions upon which aliens may enter this country, how they may acquire citizenship, and the manner in which they may be deported. Numerous treaties, in return for reciprocal promises from other governments, have pledged the solemn obligation of this nation to the end that aliens residing in our territory shall not be singled out for the imposition of discriminatory burdens. Our Constitution and our Civil Rights Act have guaranteed to aliens "the equal protection of the laws (which) is a pledge of the protection of equal laws." With a view to limiting prospective residents from foreign lands to those possessing the qualities deemed essential to good and useful citizenship in America, carefully defined qualifications are required to be met before aliens may enter our country. These qualifications include rigid requirements as to health, education, integrity, character, and adaptability to our institutions. Nor is the alien left free from the application of federal laws after entry and before naturalization. If during the time he is residing here he should be found guilty of conduct contrary to the rules and regulations laid down by Congress, he can be deported. At the time he enters the country, at the time he applies for permission to acquire the full status of citizenship, and during the intervening years, he can be subjected to searching investigations as to conduct and suitability for citizenship. And in 1940 Congress added to this comprehensive scheme a complete system for alien registration... When it made this addition to its uniform naturalization and immigration, it plainly manifested a purpose to do so in such a way as to protect the personal liberties of law-abiding aliens through one uniform national registration system, and to leave them free from the possibility of inquisitorial practices and police surveillance that might not only affect our international relations but might also generate the very disloyalty which the law has intended guarding against. Under these circumstances, the Pennsylvania Act cannot be enforced.

Accordingly, the judgment is affirmed and sustained.

NOTE:

Consider the *Issei* (Japanese settlers in the U. S.), the *Nisei* (second generation Japanese-Americans and full citizens in the U. S.), and the American Negro in light of the above case and its arguments. . .

(See *America's Concentration Camps*, a documentary by Allan R. Bosworth, New York, Norton, 1966.)

UNITED STATES v. PINK, SUPERINTENDENT OF INSURANCE, NEW YORK, 1942

United States Supreme Court

The United States initiated this action against Pink, the Superintendent of Insurance for New York State, to recover for the United States the assets of the New York branch of the First Russian Insurance Company which had remained under the administration of Pink after payment had been made to all domestic creditors and claimants in the United States.

The material background facts of the United States complaint were as follows: In 1907 the First Russian Insurance Company, organized under the laws of the former Czarist Empire, had established a branch office in New York. The Russian Insurance Company had deposited with the Superintendent of Insurance of New York State at that time certain assets which were to serve as security or collateral for claims to be transacted by the New York branch office. This procedure was pursuant (according) to the laws of New York State and provided a sound business foundation for continued operation, security and service. As a result of the Russian Revolutions of 1917, the new revolutionary Bolshevik government in 1918 and 1919 by certain laws, enactments, orders, and decrees nationalized the insurance business, among many others in Russia, and all of the Russian insurance companies, including the First Russian Insurance Company in New York.

Furthermore, this new revolutionary government discharged and cancelled all the debts of such companies and the rights of all shareholders in all such property. However, until 1925, the First Russian Insurance Company continued to do business at the New York branch office. At that time, pursuant to an order from the New York Supreme Court, the incumbent Superintendent of Insurance from New York State took possession of the assets of the New York branch of the First Russian Insurance Company for a determination and report upon the claims of the policyholders and creditors in the United States. Thereafter, the Superintendent of Insurance for New York State paid all claims of domestic creditors arising from the New York branch office and satisfied all legal obligations attendant with the branch office's operation. He was then left with a balance in his hands of more than $1,000,000, which was left to collect interest and dividends.

In 1931 the New York Court of Appeals directed the New York State Superintendent of Insurance to dispose of the balance ($1,000,000) remaining by recognizing and paying all legitimate foreign claims and creditors who had petitioned prior to the directive for redress (1931); and, if any of the balance ($1,000,000) remained after satisfying these claims and creditors, the remaining money was to be divided among the quorum of the First Russian Insurance Company's directors who were living at that time.

Before the directive ordered above could be fully accomplished the United States on November 14, 1934, initiated the aforementioned action in the Federal District Court for the Southern District of New York, seeking to recover for the U. S. the remaining assets left in the hands of the Superintendent of Insurance for New York State (see Note at end of case). As a result of appeals, which arose from unfavorable decisions in the lower level courts, the case was finally heard by the U. S. Supreme Court in 1942.

In recounting the past progress of the case from its inception in the Federal District Court for the Southern District of New York where the United States had brought action to recover the assets remaining in the hands of the respondent, Pink, that Court held that the well settled "principles governing the convenient and orderly administration of justice require that the jurisdiction of the state court should be respected"; and that, whatever might be "the effect of recognition" of the Russian Government, it did not terminate the state proceedings. The United States was remitted to the state court for determination of its claim, no opinion being intimated on the merits of the U. S. action. The United States then moved for leave to intervene in the liquidation proceedings. Its motion was denied "without prejudice to the institution of the time-honored form of action." That order was affirmed on appeal.

Thereafter, the present suit was instituted in the Supreme Court of New York. The defendants, other than respondent (Pink), were certain designated policyholders and other creditors who had presented in the liquidation proceedings claims against the corporation. The complaint prayed that the United States be adjudged to be the sole and exclusive owner entitled to immediate possession of the entire surplus fund in the hands of the respondent.

The respondent's (Pink) answer denied the allegations of the complaint that title to the funds in question passed to the United

States and that the Russian decrees had the effect claimed. It also set forth various affirmative defenses—that the order of distribution pursuant to the decree could not be affected by the Litvinov Assignment; that the Litvinov Assignment was unenforceable because it was conditioned upon a final settlement of claims and counterclaims which had not been accomplished; that under Russian law the nationalization decrees in question had no effect on property not factually taken into possession by the Russian Government prior to May 22, 1922; that the Russian decrees had no extraterritorial effect, according to Russian law; that if the decrees were given extraterritorial effect, they were confiscatory and their recognition would be unconstitutional and contrary to the public policy of the United States and of the State of New York; and that the United States, under the Litvinov Assignment, acted merely as a collection agency for the Russian Government and hence was foreclosed from asserting any title to the property in question.

In May 1939 respondent Pink filed a motion in the New York Supreme Court for a summary judgment and dismissal of the U. S. case. On June 29, 1939, the Court granted Pink's motion and dismissed the case. Appeal followed and both the Appellate Division of the New York Supreme Court (without opinion) on May 17, 1940, and the New York Court of Appeals, on December 31, 1940, affirmed the motion and summary judgment in the Pink Case. Appeal followed to the United States Supreme Court and the appeal was granted *certiorari* (a writ issued from a superior court calling up the record of a proceeding in a lower or inferior court for review) by that court.

The Supreme Court now stated that the case involved the right of the United States under the Litvinov Assignment to recover, from a custodian or stakeholder in New York, funds which had been nationalized and appropriated by the Russian decrees.

This Court held that the conduct of foreign relations is committed by the Constitution to the political departments of the Federal Government; that the propriety of the exercise of that power is not open to judicial inquiry; and that recognition of a foreign sovereign conclusively binds the courts and "is retroactive and validates all actions and conduct of the government so recognized from the commencement of its existence." It further held that recognition of the Soviet Government, the establishment of diplomatic relations with it, and the Litvinov Assignment were "all parts of one transaction, resulting in an international compact between the two governments." After stating that, "in sole organ" of the national government, it added: "The assignment and the agreements in connection therewith did not, as in the case of treaties, as that term is used in the treaty making clause of the Constitution (Art. II, sec. 2), require the advice and consent of the Senate." It held that the "external powers of the United States are to be exercised without regard to state laws or policies. The supremacy of a treaty in this respect has been recognized from the beginning." And it added that "all international compacts and agreements" are to be treated with similar dignity for the reason that "complete power over international affairs is in the national government and is not and cannot be subject to any curtailment or interference on the part of the several states."

This Court did not stop to inquire whether in fact there was any policy of New York which enforcement of the Litvinov Assignment would infringe since "no state policy can prevail against the international compact here involved."

The Court concluded that there are limitations on the sovereignty of the states. No State can rewrite our foreign policy to conform to its own domestic policies. Power over external affairs is not shared by the states; it is vested in the national government exclusively. It need not be so exercised as to conform to state laws or state policies, whether they be expressed in constitutions, statutes, or judicial decrees. And the policies of the States become wholly irrelevant to judicial inquiry when the United States, acting within its constitutional sphere, seeks enforcement of its foreign policy in the courts. The Supreme Court held that the right to the funds or property in question became vested in the Soviet Government as the successor to the First Russian Insurance Company, that this right has passed to the United States under the Litvinov Assignment, and that the United States is entitled to the property as against the corporation (insurance company) and the foreign creditors.

The judgment of the lower courts is reversed.

NOTE:

The United States recognized the Union of Socialist Soviet Republics as the *de jure* government of that geographic-political area on November 16, 1933. As an incident to that recognition, President Franklin D. Roosevelt accepted an assignment of certain claims in a letter form document which had been forwarded to the President by Maxim Litvinov, People's Commission for Foreign Affairs for the U.S.S.R. on November 16, 1933, and this document is known as the Litvinov Assignment.

THE CORFU CHANNEL CASE, 1949
United Kingdom v. Albania

International Court of Justice

On October 22, 1946, a squadron of British warships—the cruisers *Mauritius* and *Leander*, and the destroyers *Volage* and *Saumarez*— left the port of Corfu, located on the Greek island of Corfu, to perform a routine naval exercise in the Adriatic Sea. The warships had proceeded from the port of Corfu in a northward direction through the North Corfu Strait, which connected the Ionian Sea, the Straits of Otranto, and the Adriatic Sea. Following the completion of World War II in Europe, the channel of the North Corfu Strait had been swept and cleared of mines by minesweepers to enable the return of normal, peaceful commercial navigation in that area. As the British naval squadron proceeded from the port of Corfu north through the Corfu Channel and the territorial waters of Albania on the previously-stated date and mission, the destroyers *Volage* and *Saumarez* were severely damaged by striking mines which evidently had been placed in the channel by the Albanian government. The mines had been placed by the Albanian government as a result of earlier events which had occurred between the Albanian government and the British government over the use of the Corfu Channel by British naval units.

The subsequent mine explosions caused the deaths of forty-four (44) and personal injuries to forty-two (42) British officers and men of the two badly-damaged destroyers. Later, on November 13, 1946, a small fleet of British trawlers and minesweepers again swept the North Corfu Channel (in Albanian territorial waters) clear of mines and re-established peaceful, commercial navigation in that area. The minesweepers cut and removed twenty-two moored mines on this occasion and finally took two of those mines to Malta for expert examination, cataloguing and, finally, the initiation by the British government of proceedings against Albania before the International Court of Justice.

In recounting the facts which led to the final proceedings before the International Court of Justice, the dispute between Albania and the United Kingdom arose as a consequence of events which began on May 15, 1946. On that date, the British cruisers *Orion* and *Superb* were passing in a southward direction through the North Corfu Strait. In the vicinity of Saranda, Albania (opposite the Greek island of Corfu), the Albanian coastal defense battery opened fire on the southward-passing British cruisers, as the cruisers moved away from the vicinity of Saranda. The battery fired (estimate made in the report of the British commanding naval officer of May 29, 1946) from 12 to 20 rounds over a period of 12 minutes at the British cruisers as they sped southward. The Albanian coastal defense battery did not hit either of the cruisers, but the shots had come uncomfortably close. An Albanian note of May 21, 1946, stated that their Coastal Defense Commander had ordered a few shots to be fired in the direction of the British cruisers "in accordance with a General Order founded on international law".

An immediate protest from the British government to the Albanian government stated that innocent passage through straits is a right recognized by international law. Albania countered that foreign warships and merchant vessels had no right to pass through Albanian territorial waters without prior notification to, and permission of, the Albanian government. After further diplomatic correspondence and non-performance by both conflicting parties, the British government on August 2, 1946, brought things to a head with a stern note by maintaining its view with regard to the right of innocent passage through straits forming routes for international maritime traffic and commerce between two parts of the high seas. A final portion of the note included a warning that, if the Albanian coastal batteries in the future opened fire on any British warship or warships passing through the Corfu Channel in either direction, the warship or warships, as the case might be, would have orders to return the Albanian fire and protect themselves.

The contents of this final note were on August 1, 1946, communicated to the British Naval Commander-in-Chief in the Mediterranean Sea by the British Admiralty. Further, the Admiralty instructed the Commander-in-Chief that British naval units were not to use the Corfu Channel until the note had been delivered and received formally by the Albanian government. On August 10, 1946, the Commander-in-Chief was informed by telegram from the Admiralty that the note had been received by the Albanian government and formally recognized. The British Commander-in-Chief was informed that he could now begin to use again the North Corfu Strait with his naval units, but only when essential to British purposes and with the naval units armament secured in the fore and aft position of non-belligerency. However, after complying with these reservations, if the Albanian coastal guns should fire upon them, they were to protect themselves by immediately returning the Albanian fire.

On September 21, 1946, the Admiralty forwarded a communique to the British Mediterranean Fleet Commander-in-Chief requesting him to furnish the following information: Had he ordered any naval units to proceed through the North Corfu Strait; and, if he had so ordered specific units, had they been molested or impeded by the Albanian authorities? Furthermore, the communique requested that, if he had not so ordered units to proceed through the North Corfu Strait, when did he propose or intend to perform an operation in that locality?

The Commander-in-Chief answered the Admiralty's communique the following day by stating that his ships had not attempted to use the Corfu Channel, but that it was his intention that the cruisers *Mauritius* and *Leander*, plus the two destroyers *Volage* and *Saumarez*, would proceed from the port of Corfu, north to the Adriatic Sea through the North Corfu Strait. It was under such recounted circumstances that the British naval squadron was ordered on October 22, 1946, to proceed to the Adriatic Sea for naval exercises, and the unfortunate destroyers *Volage* and *Saumarez* were severely damaged by striking mines with the attendant loss of lives and injuries. The British government and the Albanian government by a Special Agreement of March 25, 1948, instituted proceedings before the International Court of Justice, where the case was then heard and decided on its merits.

The World Court by a fourteen (14) to two (2) vote gives judgment that the United Kingdom did not violate the sovereignty of the People's Republic of Albania by reason of the acts of the British Navy in Albanian waters on October 22, 1946, and the World Court unanimously gives judgment that, by reason of the acts of the British Navy in Albanian waters in the course of the minesweeping operation of November 12 and 13, 1946, the United Kingdom violated the sovereignty of the People's Republic of Albania, and that this declaration by the Court constitutes in itself appropriate satisfaction. . .

NOTE:

The World Court further awarded a judgment for damages against Albania for the loss of lives, injuries, and ship damages sustained on October 22, 1946, but Albania did not heed the judgment and refused to pay; Britain did not force the judgment award.

CARRERA v. CARRERA, 1949

United States Court of Appeals, District of Columbia Circuit

This case arose from action initiated by Rosa H. Carrera against her husband, Amable Hidalgo Carrera, for separate maintenance for herself and for support of and custody of the 15-year-old son of the parties involved in the litigation. The United States District Court for the District of Columbia first heard the case and the supporting arguments. It dismissed the complaint of Rosa H. Carrera, and as a result of this action the plaintiff, Rosa H. Carrera, appealed to the United States Court of Appeals, District of Columbia Circuit, where the case was again presented.

Both Rosa H. Carrera and Amable H. Carrera were nationals from the South American state of Ecuador and permanent residents of the United States. Both Mr. and Mrs. Carrera were domestic employees in the Embassy of Czechoslovakia when action was instituted by Rosa H. Carrera.

Amable H. Carrera moved to quash (stop completely) the serving of process upon him, and he also moved to have the complaint dismissed. He claimed diplomatic immunity from the instituted action by his wife, Rosa. Also, the Ambassador of Czechoslovakia had requested in a written communication to the Secretary of State that Amable Carrera be granted diplomatic immunity. The written evidence of this fact was enclosed in a note to the judge of the district court by the legal adviser of the Secretary of State which was admitted as evidence. It not only requested diplomatic immunity for Amable H. Carrera, but this note certified that Mr. Carrera was registered in the Department of State in accordance with required United States statutes or laws, and that his name had been included in the "White List" which was a composite record of all of the employees working in the Embassies and Legations in Washington, D. C. The note finally requested the District Court to be appreciative of these facts and take such action as it deemed to be necessary in the attendant circumstances.

The District Court then dismissed the complaint of Rosa H. Carrera on the ground that her husband Amable H. Carrera was clothed with diplomatic immunity. Rosa then appealed the case to the higher court of appeals for the District of Columbia.

The plaintiff, Rosa Carrera, based her appeal and sought reversal on several grounds: her first ground was that the right of the appellee (Amable H. Carrera) to diplomatic immunity was not properly presented to the District Court. However, the Court found that the process by which the claim of immunity was made by the Czechoslovakian Ambassador to the State Department was communicated to the court in a manner approved by the Supreme Court in the case *In Re Biaz, 1890.* It is enough that an ambassador has requested immunity, that the State Department has recognized that the person for whom it is requested is entitled to it, and that the State Department's recognition had been communicated to the Court and accepted by the Court. The plaintiff next contended that the inclusion of Mr. Carrera's name on the so-called "White List" was not sufficient to bring him within the required protection of diplomatic immunity. The Court answered that the State Department and the Secretary of State had certified Mr. Carrera's name on the list, and it was not the function of the Court to review this certification by judicial inquiry. The final contention of the plaintiff is that the rule of diplomatic immunity does not apply in the field of domestic relations. The Court stated that the question of diplomatic immunity was not raised in this case.

The Court concluded that they had no doubt that the case was properly decided by the District Court.

Dismissal was affirmed.

BERNADOTTE and OTHERS, 1949

International Court of Justice
(Advisory Opinion)

Count Folke Bernadotte, Swedish internationalist and nephew of King Gustavus V of Sweden, was appointed by the Security Council of the United Nations to act as mediator in the hostilities between the Jewish and Arab groups during the formative period of the new state of Israel. On September 17, 1948, Count Bernadotte and Colonel Andre Serat, Chief of the French U. N. Observers, were assassinated in the Israeli-held sector of Jerusalem by a fanatical, irregular band of Israeli. The tragic act led to the following Resolution adopted by the General Assembly of the United Nations on December 3, 1948, and a stated request for an advisory opinion of the International Court of Justice concerning claim reparations by the U. N. for injuries suffered by U. N. personnel in U. N. service.

The Resolution was adopted as follows:

"Whereas the series of tragic events which have lately befallen agents of the United Nations engaged in the performance of their duties raises, with greater urgency than ever, the question of the arrangements to be made by the United Nations with a view to ensuring to its agents the fullest measure of protection in the future and ensuring that reparation be made for the injuries suffered, and. . .

"Whereas it is highly desirable that the Secretary-General should be able to act without question as efficaciously as possible with a view to obtaining any reparation due; therefore. . .

The General Assembly

Decides to submit the following legal questions to the International Court of Justice for an advisory opinion:

I. In the event of an agent of the United Nations in the performance of his duties suffering injury in circumstances involving the responsibility of a State, has the United Nations, as an organization, the capacity to bring an international claim against the responsible *de jure* or *de facto* government with a view to obtaining the reparation due in respect of the damage caused (a) to the United Nations, (b) to the victim or to persons entitled through him?

II. In the event of an affirmative reply on point I (b), how is action by the United Nations to be reconciled with such rights as may be possessed by the State of which the victim is a national?"

On April 11, 1949, after exploring and arguing the various issues involved in reaching a decision, the Court did render an advisory opinion. Some of the very important notions of the Court are recounted as follows:

The Court stated that its basis for jurisdiction was founded on Article 96 (1) of the Charter of the United Nations, and Article 65 (1) of the Statute of the International Court of Justice. In answering Question #1, the Court recognized that, up until the present question had been brought before the Court, the capacity to press international claims had been considered a right and function of the States exclusively. Now the Court indicated and affirmed that the U. N., as an organization, did have the capacity to bring an international claim for reparations against the responsible *de jure* or *de facto* government involved for damages sustained. The Court did not conclude, however, that the U. N. was a State, in the traditional characteristic posture of a State, but that the extension of such capacity to the U. N. was consistent with its international political function and status and with the purpose of the rule proposed. Furthermore, the Court concluded that the U. N. could be regarded as a subject of international law for certain extenuating circumstances and purposes.

The Court then found, on a unanimous basis, in answering Question #1 (a), that the U. N. as an Organization has the capacity to bring an international claim against one of its members which has caused injury to it by a breach of its international obligations toward the Organization.

Concerning Question I (b), the Court, by 11 votes to 4, answered in the affirmative. The Court concluded that the U. N. as an Organization had a capacity to exercise a measure of functional protection for its duly appointed representatives. Thus, if a member State neglects its obligation or does not exercise due diligence, and a U. N. agent is injured or suffers damages, the U. N. is entitled to claim redress. In doing so, the U. N. is invoking its own right, the obligation by the member State is to that right, and it must be respected.

The Court continued that, even if the Sate involved in the claim was not a member State of the Organization, the international community, by its majority consensus and membership in the U.N., had the power in conformity with international law to introduce an entity possessing an objective international personality, and that personality would have the capacity to initiate international claims.

The Court answered Question #II by reaching the following conclusions on a 10 votes to 5 basis. The Court concluded:

"It is conceivable that, if the victim concerned is not state-less but has a nationality of his own, a competition might arise between his State's right of diplomatic protection and the Organization's right of functional protection. There is no rule of law that grants priority to either side. However, Article 2 (5) of the Charter emphasizes the duty of member States to render assistance to the Organization while general and particular conventions may reduce or eliminate the above-mentioned competition."

"What would be the situation if the victim was a national of the defendant State? In the light of the above consider-ations, this question is irrelevant, since the Organization's right to claim damages does not result from the nationality of the victim, but rather from his status as agent of the Organization."

The Court advisory opinion affirmed the questions presented by the Resolution of the General Assembly.

NOTE:

On the basis of the Advisory Opinion rendered by the Court, the Secretary-General in 1950 reported to the General Assembly that he had contacted by letter the Minister for Foreign Affairs of Israel. He stated that he had requested a formal apology from Israel to the U. N., the sum of $54,628 as reparations ($28,040 for funeral expenses and $26,588 for administration expenses) and the con-tinuing efforts by the Israeli government to apprehend and bring to justice the perpetrators of the crime. In due time a remittance for $54,628 was forthcoming from the Israeli government, an apology for what had happened, and the continuing efforts of the Israeli to bring the culprits to justice was indicated. However, Israel never admitted the legal contentions made were valid.

SEE: Sohn, *Cases and Materials on United Nations Law*, pp. 249-270.

Syatauw, *Decisions of the International Court of Justice*, pp. 168-172.

UNITED STATES v. COPLON and GUBITCHEV, 1950

United States District Court, S.D.N.Y.

This case arose as both Judith Coplon and Valentine A. Gubitchev were indicted for conspiracy to violate and for the actual violation of United States espionage laws. Miss Coplon was an employee of the United States Department of Justice, and Mr. Gubitchev was an employee of the United Nations Secretariat. Both Miss Coplon and Mr. Gubitchev were arrested on March 4, 1949, and on March 10, 1949, they were indicted on the above-stated charges. Mr. Gubitchev refused to plead and claimed "diplomatic immunity". The Court then examined the question of his diplomatic immunity and held, on May 10, 1949, that "the defendant is not a public minister, that he (Gubitchev) does not possess 'diplomatic immunity' ". The court then concluded that it had jurisdiction in this case and could render a binding decision.

The Court argued that as Gubitchev had engaged in allegedly unlawful activities and that, as these activities has been directed against the United States government, the nature of the charges directed against Gubitchev were very serious. Furthermore, the court continued by stating that Gubitchev's activities were liable to endanger United States security and that this, in turn, could be reflected in the United States peaceful relations with other states.

Historically, in the past, the United States Department of State has had to make foreign governments aware by reminding them that, even if they have the right through comity to use as a defense basis in litigation the concept of "diplomatic immunity", they should not, under the Law of Nations (International Law) use such a defense media in impeding the natural course of justice or even permit such privileges to develop as a shield from punishment for the perpetrator or perpetrators of crimes of the type charged above.

Gubitchev and his defense counsel readily conceded that he was not a diplomatic officer of the U.S.S.R. and attached to the Soviet Embassy. Furthermore, Gibutchev recalled that he was never officially received nor accredited by our government.

He also conceded that he had not been sent to this country. However, in his motion, Gubitchev did remind the Court that he was a diplomatic officer of the U.S.S.R., that he had come to this country to accept and occupy a position with the United Nations Secretariat, that he had in his possession a diplomatic passport issued by the U.S.S.R.'s Ministry of Foreign Affairs and a diplomatic visa issued by the United States Embassy in Moscow. Therefore, under the Law of Nations (International Law) Gubitchev concluded that he is entitled to recognition of diplomatic status with all its attendant immunities and privileges, including in this case being free from prosecution on the charges herein presented. Gubitchev then entertained the motion that he be discharged from the indictment for conspiracy to violate and for the violation of U. S. espionage laws.

The District Court recounted some of the facts by stating that the Court concludes that the defendant's motion must be denied on the following premises: Gubitchev's claim of immunity is grounded solely on the facts that he is a diplomatic officer of the U.S.S.R., that he was, in this capacity, sent by his government to the United Nations and that he was in possession of a diplomatic passport and diplomatic visa at the time of his arrest. It has been long recognized that the United States will not afford diplomatic immunity unless the person claiming it not only has diplomatic status, but is also in an intimate association with the work of a permanent diplomatic mission.

In this case, tried on its merits, the defendant has never asserted that he came to this country on a diplomatic mission, and evidence supports that he never acted in a diplomatic character in the United States. The visa and passport, which were affixed to the defendant's passport, did not of themselves constitute a grant of diplomatic immunity for all of his activities in this country. The Department of State further certifies that the defendant does not enjoy diplomatic status.

Diplomatic status is a political question and a matter of state; the finding of the Secretary of State must be accepted unquestioned by this Court. Therefore, the Court concluded that Gubitchev was possessed of none of the prerogatives of a diplomat and was cloaked with no immunity from prosecution in this country for the acts charged against him.

The motion is denied and Gubitchev remained as charged. He and Miss Coplon were convicted.

NOTE:

On March 9, 1950, Valentine Gubitchev and Judith Coplon were sentenced as spies to 15 years in prison. On recommendation of the Departments of State and Justice, Gubitchev's sentence was suspended on the condition that he leave the United States "never to return".

PORTUGAL v. INDIA, 1960

International Court of Justice

This case arose as a result of an insurrection in 1954 which erupted in the inland Portuguese enclaves of Dadra and Nagar-Aveli, located on the sub-continent of India, north of the city of Bombay. From the time in which the Portuguese had landed (1498) and established trading posts on the Malabar coast (west coast) of India, she had exercised sovereign control over her enclaves in that area, and the various preceding governments in India, as well as the present Indian government, had permitted this action to evolve and continue. The Portuguese enclaves through which Portuguese sovereignty had been implemented are as follows: Damao, Diu, and Goa, which were located on the Malabar coast of India, and the small inland enclaves of Dadra and Nagar-Aveli. Due to the insurrection which arose in the two inland enclaves of Dadra and Nagar-Aveli, and the state of tension created by the insurrection, the government of India prohibited the passage of Portuguese officials and troops from the coastal enclave of Damao to the two involved inland enclaves of the Portuguese. Portugal then initiated proceedings before the World Court on December 22, 1955, stating that India's action deprived Portugal of the right of passage to maintain law and order and to exercise her sovereign rights and obligations in the two affected enclaves.

The World Court adjudged that Portugal in 1954 had a right of passage over the intervening Indian territory between Damao and their turbulent enclaves of Dadra and Nagar-Aveli to the extent necessary for the exercise of Portuguese sovereignty, but that this right of passage was subject to the control and the regulation of the Republic of India. Thus, India could distinguish between the passage of private persons, civil officials, merchandise, armed forces, armed police, and arms and ammunition. However, the Court held that India had no right to intervene in the insurrections with Indian forces or use them to deter Portugal in maintaining her sovereignty in the enclaves.

In referring back to the specific complaint by Portugal of the Indian refusal to permit the delegates of the Portuguese governor of Damao to visit the disturbed enclaves, the Court held that India had "not acted in violation of its obligation resulting from Portugal's right of passage", since this refusal was covered by India's admitted power of regulating the passage of civilian personnel. Furthermore, it was justified by the tension created in the Indian territory adjacent to the turbulent enclaves. The judgment of the World Court technically confirmed Portugal's "right of passage" and right to exercise its sovereignty in the enclaves, but the Court refused to consider the larger issues of India's role in instigating the insurrections in the enclaves and the legality of India's restrictions on the passage of the Portuguese civil officials, which in reality hampered and limited Portugal from exercising and maintaining sovereignty in the enclaves.

Portugal obtained moral but not practical satisfaction from the World Court. It was a hollow victory for Portugal.

HONDURAS v. NICARAGUA, 1960

International Court of Justice

Involved in this dispute was a sector of the Mosquito Coast, a thinly-populated area of approximately 300 square miles, which is located along the boundary of the contesting countries. Both countries have long proclaimed sovereignty over the area.

In retrospect, on October 7, 1894, the Gamez-Bonilla Treaty between Honduras and Nicaragua was concluded, which sought to settle the dispute over the contested Mosquito coast area. In 1900 a mixed commission from both countries established the frontier boundary from the Pacific coast area to a point adjacent to the present contested area, namely, Portillo de Teotecacinte, but from this point eastward to the Caribbean coast the mixed commission was unable to agree and establish a mutually agreeable frontier boundary. On October 4, 1904, both Honduras and Nicaragua agreed to petition and request the King of Spain, Alfonso XIII (1902-1931), to decide the controversy over the disputed area. The Spanish monarch fulfilled their request and made his arbitral award on December 23, 1906, in favor of Honduras.

Even though the award was accepted by both Honduras and Nicaragua, it was not implemented and fulfilled by Nicaragua. Six years later, on March 19, 1912, Nicaragua formally challenged the validity of the Spanish monarch's award to Honduras. At this juncture, the United States tendered its good offices in order to resolve the newly-emerging aspects of the old dispute, and the United States failed to resolve the difficulty. In 1957 the question of the disputed area was referred to the Organization of American States for consultation and advice. As a result of this development, an agreement was finally arrived at in Washington, D. C., on July 21, 1957, between Honduras and Nicaragua to refer the dispute to the World Court at The Hague, Netherlands.

Nicaragua based its arguments before the World Court on the following issues: They argued that the Spanish king had been improperly designated as arbitrator, that he had exceeded his powers, that his award was vitiated by serious error, and that the execution of the award was not possible due to many obscurities, omissions, and contradictions involved in said award. Honduras, of course, claimed that the award of the Spanish king was valid, and as a result of Nicaraguan acceptance at the time of the award, compliance and obligation should be forthcoming by Nicaragua.

The World Court rejected Nicaragua's contentions by stating the following arguments: Inasmuch as Nicaragua failed to challenge the regularity of the award and designation of King Alfonso XIII of Spain at the time, 1904-06, and Nicaragua had participated in the arbitral proceedings, they (Nicaragua) at this time could not challenge the proceedings and thus were precluded from doing so by a past, tacit consent. The Court continued rejecting the defendant's contentions by further stating that Nicaragua had not presented convincing proof that there were obscurities, omissions, errors, and contradictions in the award; and finally, Nicaragua, by accepting the award, precluded any opportunity she might have of going back on her earlier recognition of it.

In this case, the Court refused to act as a Court of Appeal and did not examine whether the award was right or wrong, but merely took time to review the grounds of nullity submitted by Nicaragua. The major basis upon which the Court rendered its decision was predicated upon the earlier acceptance of arbitration and Nicaragua's acceptance at that time of the award, 1906.

The World Court then ruled in favor of Honduras.

ISRAEL v. EICHMANN, 1962

District Court of Jerusalem

On April 11, 1961, before a three-judge district court in Jerusalem, Israel, the trial of defendant, Adolf Eichmann, former head of the Gestapo's Jewish Affairs Bureau in Hitler's Third Reich during World War II, was convened and opened. The trial was given world-wide coverage by all communications media available at that time. The case involved and exposed for world-wide consumption the planned liquidation of millions of Jews (6,000,000) by the Nazis. Thus, the legal issues, while important, were, in a sense, subordinated to the overriding moral obligations involved, and a great deal of controversy and debate was touched off by this case.

Some of the major legal points touched upon were as follows: First, the question of universal jurisdiction arose: did an Israeli court have jurisdiction over a foreigner (non-citizen) who had committed crimes in a foreign nation-state? Second, could an Israeli court try an individual foreigner under the principle of universal jurisdiction who had been brought before their district court by abduction, espionage, and the violation of the territorial sovereign rights of another nation-state? Third, could the defendant be tried by a retroactive statute which had been passed in 1950, quite a number of years after the crimes had been committed? And, finally, could an Israeli court of justice be objective toward the crime of genocide?

The question of the retroactive statute and its application was covered by the plaintiff very rapidly and easily by pointing back to the precedents established and settled by the Nuremberg War Crimes' Trials following World War II in 1945 and 1946, which developed from the London Agreement of 1945.

The abduction argument was also met with and resolved in the due course of events, but not too convincingly. Gideon Hausner, the attorney-general of Israel and chief prosecutor for the plaintiff, cited instances in British and American legal cases which established the right and competency of a court to try a defendant, maintaining that the manner or method in which the defendant reached the court's jurisdiction was irrelevant.

The initial question of jurisdiction of the district court was a difficult one to answer, because the violation of the principle of territoriality in international law permits only one exception, namely, the act and crime of piracy. Under the crime of piracy, an individual so accused may be tried by any state which apprehends the individual, and the so-called doctrine of universal jurisdiction would apply. However, the crime of piracy proved to be somewhat of a problem, since acts of piracy are normally committed on the high seas; and, as a consequence of that geographic location, the evidence to support the crime of piracy is normally available at the time of the apprehending of the culprit or culprits. In the case of the defendant, differences appeared: The defendant had not committed his crimes on the high seas, but in a number of middle European countries, namely, Austria, Hungary, Poland, Germany, and a number of others. The analogy drawn in this case between genocide and piracy was not new. For example, the Genocide Convention, whose resolutions were adopted by the U. N. General Assembly December 9, 1948, very clearly rejected the claim to universal jurisdiction and stated instead that "persons charged with genocide. . .shall be tried by a competent tribunal of the States in the territory of which the act was committed or by such international penal tribunal as may have jurisdiction". Confronted with a very sticky legal problem in this area with the principal of universal jurisdiction and violation of a state's territoriality, the plaintiff finally resolved the issues on the grounds that the Jewish state of Israel, by its uniqueness as being a haven for Jews who escaped the Nazi extermination resolution of the Wannsee Conference, January 1942, had in effect derived a special right to jurisdiction over the defendant who had been designated as the chief exterminator by the Nazis at the Wannsee Conference. Furthermore, if that special uniqueness of the Jewish posture was not sufficient to merit universal jurisdiction, the crimes of the defendant alone warranted universal jurisdiction. The problem of infringing upon and violating the sovereign territorial rights of Argentian was solved by the joint declaration of Israel and Argentina on August 3, 1960, which stated that they "resolved to view as settled the incident which was caused in the wake of the action of citizens of Israel which violated the basic rights of the State of Argentina". Actually, Argentina ran contrary to her usual mode of behavior at this time (she had given sanctuary and asylum to a number of ex-Nazis), due, no doubt, to the magnitude of the case and world opinion. Also, the fact that the defendant was not a citizen of Argentina, but in a sense was almost stateless since the fall of the Third Reich, reduced the tension. The fact that the defendant had not requested asylum from Argentina was a further inhibition to Argentina.

The question as to whether an Israeli court of justice could be objective toward the defendant was answered, again shakily from a legal standpoint, by the application of the passive-personality principle (no emotion; complete objectivity) which the plaintiff assured the defendant would be invoked. In other words, the Court assured the defendant that they would and could be objective and rational in his case. Thus, the outstanding legal issues were answered in the manner indicated.

On December 11, 1961, the District Court of Jerusalem, after due deliberation, found the defendant guilty of crimes against the Jewish people, crimes against humanity, war crimes, and other crimes. On December 15 the defendant was sentenced to death by hanging. However, the District Court stated that the defendant had the right to appeal both the judgment of guilty and the sentence of hanging before the Supreme Court of Israel.

The defendant appealed. On March 22, 1962, review proceedings were initiated before the Supreme Court of Israel. On May 29, 1962, the Supreme Court of Israel upheld the judgment and sentence of the defendant by the District Court. A final personal plea for mercy by the defendant to the President of Israel was rejected.

On May 31, 1962, Adolf Eichmann, the defendant, was hanged until dead, cremated, and his ashes scattered in the Mediterranean Sea off the Israel shore. His final words were: "Long live Germany, long live Argentina, long live Austria. I shall not forget them."

CAMBODIA v. THAILAND, 1962

International Court of Justice

The dispute upon which this case was founded emerged as a result of the contention by both Cambodia and Thailand that each had sovereignty over the area encompassing the ancient and famous Temple of Preah Vihear. The ruins of this noted temple are situated in the Dangrek mountain range, which extend along the Cambodian-Thailand border, and due to past frontier indecision the temple became a focal point of tension between Cambodia (formerly, part of French Indo-China) and Thailand (formerly Siam). In February 1904 France, who controlled Indo-China, and Siam, now Thailand, concluded a boundary treaty providing that in the Dangrek mountain sector the boundary should follow the watershed line. Furthermore, it was agreed that a mixed commission should actually determine the frontier on the specific ground area. Eventually, maps were prepared by the French authorities upon the request and assent of the Siamese commission to facilitate this project. Unfortunately, these maps were not submitted in time to the mixed commission. which had proceeded to disband. Consequently, these maps were construed not to be of a binding nature at that time.

In 1908 copies of these maps were forwarded to Siam. The map upon which the present disputed temple area was projected showed the Preah Vihear temple area to be in Cambodia, although this boundary line did not follow the earlier indicated watershed line. Subsequently, Siam (Thailand) failed to avail itself of a number of opportunities to challenge these maps and the subsequent sovereign hegemony of French Indo-China and, after 1954, Cambodia over the temple area. However, during the ensuing half-century, from 1904 to the present, Thailand has stationed keepers and policemen at the temple area which Cambodia contends is an infringement of her sovereign rights. The present case arose from these conflicting elements of an improper frontier boundary and violation of Cambodian sovereignty.

Cambodia accepted the jurisdiction of the World Court pursuant to Article 36, paragraph 2, of the World Court Statute by an open declaration on September 9, 1957. Thailand contended that her earlier declarations of compulsory jurisdictional acceptance by the

Court were not valid. Thailand claimed that her declaration of May 3, 1940, and earlier declaration of September 20, 1929, admitting acceptance of compulsory Permanent Court jurisdiction were cancelled and allowed to lapse when, in April of 1946, the original Permanent Court of the old League of Nations had ceased to exist, and the new World Court of the United Nations emerged. The defendant (Thailand) further claimed that, even though she had renewed on May 20, 1950, by a declaration that she would accept compulsory jurisdiction of the new World Court, this renewal was meaningless and invalid, since the old Court had ceased to exist in 1946 and she did not feel bound by this new declaration of 1950. Furthermore, Thailand continued that she had been exercising sovereign authority in the temple area for over a long period, and on this basis alone the question of sovereignty should not arise.

The World Court then began dismissing the contentions of Thailand by pointing out these facts: The Court maintained that Thailand's sovereignty over the temple area had been performed by local, minor officials, and this did not constitute sovereignty; but, even more importantly, Thailand had on numerous occasions passed up opportunities to challenge the boundary indicated on the early maps drawn in 1904-08. France in 1930, 1949, and 1950 asserted sovereignty over the temple area, and in 1953 and 1954 Cambodia questioned the presence of Thai policemen and keepers and requested their withdrawal. At no time during these earlier developments did Thailand raise or pursue a claim through its diplomatic channels. The Court also contended that Thailand's declaration of compulsory acceptance of World Court jurisdiction in 1950 was valid. The Court held that Thailand was precluded by its own conduct from pleading error with regard to the early map drawn up; that by its past actions it indicated consent of the line drawn on that map; that the temple area boundary had enjoyed 50 years of benefits as a stable frontier. Thus, Thailand could not now challenge these developments; that both parties on this basis had accepted the early established boundary line and fulfilled the terms of the treaty; and that, as a result of these past developments, their conduct (Thailand and Cambodia) superceded the watershed line provided for in the treaty of 1904.

The Court, by a vote of 9 to 3, ruled that the temple was situated in territory under Cambodia's sovereignty and that Thailand was obligated to remove its police forces and keepers from that area.

The Court, by a vote of 7 to 5, ruled that Thailand was obligated to return to Cambodia any sculptures, fragments, and ancient pottery that may have been removed from the area after 1954.

NOTE:

In this case the World Court pointed out that the chief objective of a boundary settlement is to establish certainty and finality of a boundary and to do so by natural and visible lines. Thus, the line on the early map, even though it did not follow the watershed line, fulfilled the certainty and finality necessary to fulfill a stability requirement. The intent of the early treaty (1904) was then fulfilled and requirements met. The judgment was accepted by Thailand and executed by them.

CAMEROON v. UNITED KINGDOM, 1963

International Court of Justice

The Republic of Cameroon's complaint against the United Kingdom arose from certain related aspects of the United Kingdon's administration of the former trust territory of the Cameroons. To facilitate the administration of the territory, Britain had divided the area into northern and southern regions, known as the Southern Cameroons and the Northern Cameroons. The Northern region was administered under the protectorate of the British in the north region of Nigeria, and the Southern region under the administration of the eastern region of Nigeria. The General Assembly of the U. N. had recommended in 1959 that separate plebiscites be held in the two parts of the Cameroons' territory to determine the wishes of their electorates concerning their future political evolution.

In February 1961, the South Cameroons held its plebiscite and registered the wish of its inhabitants to achieve their independence by joining the Republic of the Cameroon. Later, in 1961, the General Assembly then decided that the Southern Cameroons should join the Republic of the Cameroon during October 1961.

The inhabitants of the Northern Cameroon had indicated by plebiscite in 1959 that at a designated future date they would decide with which area they desired to be incorporated. As a result of this impasse, the General Assembly recommended that a second and deciding plebiscite be held and the inhabitants be given the choice of achieving independence by joining either the Republic of Cameroon or the Federation of Nigeria. Concurrently, the General Assembly recommended that the United Kingdom implement steps to separate the administration of the Northern Cameroons from the Federation of Nigeria by October 1960.

In February 1961, the second plebiscite was held and the electorate of the Northern Cameroons indicated their desire to join Nigeria. This result was endorsed by the General Assembly in April 1961, and the General Assembly further decided that the trusteeship agreement between Nigeria and the Northern Cameroons be terminated on June 1, 1961, when upon that date the joining of Nigeria and the Northern Cameroons would take place.

The failure of the United Kingdom to accomplish the administrative separation of Northern Cameroons from Nigeria prior to the plebiscite, along with other objections to its administration of the trust territory, formed the substance of the Republic of the Cameroons' complaint before the World Court. The Republic of the Cameroon believed that, if the trust territory in question had been properly administered by the United Kingdom and if the recommendation by the General Assembly concerning plebiscite dates had been brought about as specified, the result of the plebiscite in Northern Cameroon would have been in favor of the Republic of the Cameroon. Complicating the case was the trusteeship agreement between Nigeria and the Northern Cameroon which had placed the United Kingdom as trustee for the Cameroons' area, and this trusteeship agreement was still valid on May 30, 1961, when the Republic of Cameroon applied to the World Court to have its complaints adjudicated. This trusteeship was not to be terminated until June 1, 1961, in accordance with the resolution that had been adopted by the U. N. General Assembly the previous April 21, 1961.

In this case the World Court handed down a most unusual judgment as a result of the conflicting facts involved. The Court in this case was satisfied that, in the preliminary stage of the case, circumstances had arisen since Cameroon filed its complaint on May 30, 1961, "to render any adjudication devoid of purpose" and that "any judgment which the Court might pronounce would be without object". The Court found that the judicial function requires that these exist not merely at the time of application of the complaint but also "at the time of the adjudication and introductory proceedings an actual controversy involving a conflict of legal interests between the parties."

The World Court, for the first time, by a vote of 10 to 5, found that it could not adjudicate upon the merits in this case due to the change in circumstances between the complaint filing time and the preliminary hearings. The Court recognized its duty to adjudicate upon disputes duly submitted to it, but the Court further indicated its overriding "duty to safeguard the judicial function" by not involving itself with political problems which could be solved by diplomatic means between states.

The Court declined jurisdiction.

SHIMODA and OTHERS v. JAPAN

Tokyo District Court, December 7, 1963

This case was initiated by a group of injured Japanese survivors from the United States atomic attacks on the Japanese cities of Hiroshima and Nagasaki. The attacks had occurred on August 6, 1945, on Hiroshima and on August 9, 1945, on Nagasaki with a tremendous loss of civilian lives, property, bodily injuries, radiation effects, and a new type of burn caused by the bomb. Interestingly enough, the Tokyo District Court handed down its decision on December 7, 1963, just twenty-two years after the Japanese attack on Pearl Harbor, Hawaii.

In recounting the facts of the atomic bombings and their effects upon the two Japanese cities involved, the tragedy evolved as follows: Early on Monday morning at about 8:15 A.M. (some sources indicate 9:15 A.M.) on August 6, 1945, a new weapon of warfare was introduced by the United States. This new weapon was called an "atomic bomb", and it was dropped by a United States Air Force B-29 bomber (the *ENOLA GAY*) under the command of its pilot, Colonel Paul W. Tibbets, Jr.; the bombardier was Major Thomas W. Ferebee, and the accompanying crew member who armed the device was Captain Parsons who had earlier helped design the bomb. The final approval and orders to drop the atomic bomb had been issued by President Harry S. Truman en route home from the Potsdam Conference which had been held in Germany. The bomb dropped on Hiroshima exploded above-ground in the air and a terrific flash and ball of fire emerged. Buildings collapsed or were swept away by the bomb's devastating effects, thousands perished, and thousands were maimed and injured. . .some with horrible burns, others with radiation effects which showed up in varying degrees and side effects over a period of days, months, and even years. Over 4.1 square miles of the center of Hiroshima were devastated and flattened by the effects of this one atomic bomb.

The following Thursday, August 9, 1945, another "atomic bomb" was dropped on the city of Nagasaki about 11:02 A.M. (Some sources indicate the time as being about 12:01 P.M.) The B-29 bomber (the *Great Artiste*, in this instance) was piloted by Major Charles W. Sweeney; and, as in the case of Hiroshima, the atomic bomb dropped wrought extreme havoc in the city of Nagasaki. Even though the bomb dropped on Nagasaki was an improved model over its predecessor used at Hiroshima, the collective losses at Nagasaki were not as great as at Hiroshima, due to a smaller city population, geographic circumstances, and a lower level of detonation by the bomb.

The case itself presented a number of unique areas for judicial inquiry and argumentation. Japan, by adhering to the doctrine of incorporation, recognized public international law (customary and positive international law consisting of customs and treaties) as part of the basic municipal law of Japan; and, hence, an individual could seek and claim redress for damages under their municipal law for an overt international act. The treaty made effective between the United States and Japan on April 28, 1952, by exchange of waivers of responsibility made both the United States and Japan responsible for caring for injuries sustained and settling claims for damages received during the conflict. Thus, Japan, by this waiver, assumed responsibility for all damages inflicted upon the Japanese people and Japan by the United States; and, correspondingly, the United States by waiver assumed responsibility for all injuries, claims, and damages inflicted upon Americans and the United States by Japan. The treaty, which became effective on April 28, 1952, and was concluded on September 8, 1958, then had the full force of law in both lands. One of the plaintiff's (Shimoda and Others) contentions was that it was illegal for Japan to waive those municipal law claims under the terms of the treaty with the United States; and, as a consequence, she (Japan) then assumed the responsibility under the Japanese State Compensation Law to remit damages to the plaintiffs because of their illegal waiving of responsibility in the Treaty with the United States. The problem of diplomatic protection[1] was explored, the legal theory in the United States of so-called sovereign immunity[2] was evaluated, as was the Act of State[3] versus fundamental human rights, with the conclusion that, in the United States, recourse would be difficult because in cases of this type, judicial review at the municipal level is limited by the important considerations of international political power (Article 6, Paragraph 2, of Federal Constitution) and the executive branch of government.

1. One state may demand from another state reparations for damage caused to its nationals, in the name of the state for the sake of the nationals.
2. The state does not accept responsibility of compensation for illegal acts committed by public servants in performance of their duty.
3. Judicial review does not intervene in the conflict—a political basis only for settlement.

The plaintiffs (Shimoda and others) presented some very interesting contentions in their claims for damages concerning the implications of Hiroshima and Nagasaki. First, they maintained that the dropping of the atomic bombs was an extremely hostile act taken by the United States, even though a state of war existed between the United States and the Japanese Empire. This hostile act, they stated, was construed to be an illegal act of hostility which was contrary to the established positive international law (treaties and customary laws) of that period of time. The plaintiffs then proceeded to cite from the following past sources pertaining to the rules and regulation of warfare: the St. Petersburg Declaration of December 11, 1868; the Hague Regulations of 1899, pertaining to the Laws and Customs of War on Land; the Hague Declaration of 1907 (Second Hague Conference); the Geneva Protocol of 1925; the Draft Rules of Air Warfare adopted in 1923; and, finally, the Convention on the Prevention and Punishment of Genocide which was adopted by the United Nations General Assembly in 1948. The plaintiffs concluded their first body of contentions by stating that, even if the aforementioned positive international law (treaties and customary laws) does not directly apply in this case, their spirit (moral and ethical effect) must be said to have the effect of natural law or logical international law. Second, the plaintiffs made especially pointed the awsome destructive power of the atomic bomb; the type of destruction wrought and injuries sustained by its use; its power political portents for future international complications; that Hiroshima and Nagasaki were not centers of war potential or military bases; that President Truman, his associates and advisers, as well as those involved in the production and research of the bomb knew its dreadful power; that the defeat of Japan was inevitable, and the bomb was used as an instrument of terror to force Japan out of the war; and, finally, that the Secretary of War, Henry Stimson, was petitioned and President Truman provided with a report by a group of scientists under the chairmanship of Professor James Frank to either abstain from using the weapon or provide Japan with notice of its potential and use; the petition and report to the Secretary of War and the President were disregarded by them and, without notice, Hiroshima and Nagasaki were bombed.

Lastly, due to the doctrine of incorporation (Japanese law and International Law were one and the same), it was not only possible to try this case on its merits under International Law, but also to try it under existing Japanese municipal law. Implied in all of the contentions of the plaintiffs was the moral and ethical consideration that the real defendant in the case was the United States and that the present Japanese state was fulfilling the role of the United States as defendant.

The defendant state (Japan) stated that atomic bombing is not necessarily contrary to international law. The state continued that, as the previously-cited conferences and agreements developing along with international law had not been concluded as a treaty at the time of the bomb's use, they cannot be recognized as part of positive international law and, as such, they cannot be made a source of international law. Therefore, the use of atomic bombs and the bombing of Hiroshima was not illegal or contrary to international law. The state further contended that, even though the act of atomic bombing may be covered by international law, it is not covered by municipal law. The U. S. legal principle of state immunity (Act of State: If a public servant of the federal or state government commits a tort (a civil wrong) in performance of his or her duties, the victim may not claim damages) was cited, which exonerated President Truman and those involved in the atomic development; the conflict of laws (conflict of jurisdiction and legal systems) was pointed out between the Japanese and American legal systems which would not readily permit access to each other and use by Japanese or American citizens. The State also cited the waiver clause in the Japanese-American Treaty, effective in 1952 and concluded in 1958, that the treaty did not waive the claims of Japanese at home or in the United States but that the plaintiffs had access to redress both within Japan and the United States by using their political or legal systems. Finally, the State concluded that the claim for compensation under the existing Japanese State Compensation Law was not made a concrete claim by the Japanese Constitution; and, thus, the claim for compensation should be dismissed.

The Tokyo District Court ruled the plaintiffs' claims improper and dismissed them on their merits. The costs of litigation shall be borne by the plaintiffs. (See Appendices I, II, and III for exhibits, notes, documents, and U.S. newspaper reports at that time., pp. 119, 120, 121, 122, 123, and 147.)

*Nagai, Takashi, *We of Nagasaki*. New York, Duell, Sloan and Pearce, March, 1964. (Foreword by Norman Cousins.)

Giovannitti, Len and Freed, Fred, *The Decision to Drop the Bomb*. New York, Coward, McCann, Inc., 1965.

BANCO NACIONAL de CUBA v. SABBATINO, 1964

United States Supreme Court

This case was heard and decided by the United States Supreme Court upon an appeal by the plaintiff from judgments rendered against the plaintiff by lower federal courts. In March 1961 the United States District Court, Southern District, New York, had heard the rather complicated litigation facts initiating this case, which had its origin in the Cuban government's resolution of August 6, 1960, signed by the Cuban President and Prime Minister, Fidel Castro, and which nationalized (expropriated) American enterprises in Cuba. The present case then developed as a consequence of the sale of a shipment of sugar that had been nationalized by the resolution of the Cuban government. The consignment of sugar had been originally owned by a subsidiary of the C.A.V. (Compania Azucarera Vertientes - Camaguey de Cuba). The C.A.V. was a corporation that had been organized under Cuban law, but whose capital stock was primarily owned by stockholders who were residents of the United States. The consignment of sugar had been sold to a New York partnership, Farr, Whitlock and Company by the C.A.V. The consignment of sugar, which had been loaded upon the S. S. *Hornfels*, a German ship at the Cuban port of Santa Maria (Juraco), was seized by the Cuban government of Fidel Castro as a result of their nationalization decree.

On August 9, 1960, after the seizure of the sugar shipment under the decree by the Cuban government, but prior to the sailing of the S. S. *Hornfels* from Cuban jurisdiction on August 11, 1960, Farr, Whitlock and Company signed a new contract with the Banco de Nacional de Cuba, a government agency representing the Castro regime. The new contract embodied similar contract terms as had been previously agreed upon with C.A.V., namely, that Farr, Whitlock would undertake to pay the Banco Nacional for the consignment of sugar cargo upon the S. S. *Hornfels* when the sugar cargo was delivered to them (Farr, Whitlock). After the delivery of the consignment of sugar, both the C.A.V. and the Banco Nacional claimed payment from the New York partnership of Farr, Whitlock and Company. Farr, Whitlock, however, was ordered not to pay the proceeds to the Banco Nacional's agent upon the basis of the new contract of August 9, 1960, since they had been advised that a receiver, Peter Sabbatino, had been appointed by the New York State Supreme Court under State statute as the legitimate receiver for C.A.V. Farr, Whitlock complied with the order of the state court and turned over to the stated receiver, Peter Sabbatino, $175,250.69, which he subsequently deposited in the King's County Trust Company until a final disposition and order for the proceeds would be made by the state court.

The plaintiff (Banco Nacional's agent in New York) then initiated proceedings in the U. S. District Court, Southern District, New York, seeking recovery of the sale proceeds ($175,250.69) from either the state court appointee Sabbatino or from Farr, Whitlock and Company.

The U. S. District Court dismissed the summary judgment and complaint of the plaintiff. The plaintiff then appealed to the U. S. Court of Appeals, Second Circuit, where on July 6, 1962, that court affirmed and upheld the judgment of the lower district court.

The plaintiff then carried and appealed the judgments of the lower courts to the United States Supreme Court where on March 23, 1964, the U. S. Supreme Court reversed the judgment of the Court of Appeals and remanded the case back to the District Court for proceedings consistent with this opinion.

Judgment reversed in favor of the plaintiff.

NOTE:

The District Court and the Court of Appeals (lower federal courts) had rejected the claim of the Cuban government (Banco Nacional) by taking the position that the immunity which is accorded through comity and sovereign rights by the courts of one state to the acts of another state within the jurisdiction of that state were subject to the condition that such acts in themselves were not contrary to international law. Consequently, the lower federal courts substantiated their rejection of the plaintiff's claim (Banco Nacional - Cuban government) by indicating that the nationalization (expropriation) of American enterprises in Cuba, though carried out within a valid Cuban jurisdiction, was in violation of international law because the act (Cuban nationalization resolution) was undertaken as a measure of retaliation in discriminating against property of American nationals, and further because adequate compensation for the expropriation of American property had not been provided.

The Supreme Court, in reversing the rulings of the lower federal courts, also indicated that the Cuban nationalization resolution

103

(expropriation) had been discriminatory, retaliatory and, in short, confiscatory. However, the Supreme Court was not willing to conclude that the Cuban government's act had been contrary to international law, but even if construed to be contrary to international law, the act of state doctrine would preclude the judgments of the lower federal courts.

Mr. Justice Harlan delivered the opinion of the Supreme Court... "The act of state doctrine in its traditional formulation precludes the courts of this country (U.S.A.) from inquiring into the validity of the public acts a recognized foreign sovereign power committed within its own territory."

The decision rendered was based upon an 8 - 1 decision in favor of the plaintiff. Mr. Justice Byron White was the lone dissenter.

For a complete coverage of the *Sabbatino* case, see *The Aftermath of Sabbatino*, Lyman M. Tondel, Jr., editor, Dobbs Ferry, N. Y., Oceana Publications, Inc., 1965.

ETHIOPIA and LIBERIA v. SOUTH AFRICA, 1966

International Court of Justice

This case had its origins in the U. N. General Assembly, which since 1946 had urged the former Union of South Africa, since 1961 the Republic of South Africa, to submit annual reports on its administration of the mandate over South West Africa (formerly, German South West Africa prior to World War I). This mandate had been conferred upon the former Union of South Africa by resolution and the mandate system of the League of Nations Council on December 17, 1920 (see Article 22, League of Nations Covenant). The U. N. General Assembly had urged South Africa to accept its supervision over the administration of the territory in accordance with the advisory opinion delivered by the World Court on July 11, 1950. The U. N. General Assembly further enjoined and strengthened the World Court advisory opinion by its resolutions 1361 (XIV) and 1565 (XV) of November 17, 1959, and December 18, 1960, which stated that the dispute over the mandate and its attendant problems be referred to the World Court for adjudication, since it appeared that negotiation could not settle this dispute. Both Liberia and Ethiopia were commended and lauded for their initiative in bringing the dispute before the World Court for review.

In due form, then, with resolution 1361 (XIV), both Ethiopia and Liberia, by concurrent (together, as one) application initiated proceedings against South Africa on November 4, 1960, which referred to the duties and performance of South Africa in its status as mandatory for South West Africa. Liberia and Ethiopia charged violations of the terms and objectives of the mandate committed by the mandatory, specifically, by practicing *apartheid* (separate development of racial groups), failing to promote to the utmost the material and moral well-being of the inhabitants, and impeding opportunities for self-determination by the peoples of the mandated area. The applicant states (Liberia and Ethiopia) based the jurisdiction of the court on Article 7, Paragraph 2, of the mandate, and Article 37 of the Statute of the World Court. The former Union of South Africa on November 30, 1960, filed four (4) preliminary objections to the jurisdiction of the World Court, and the Court on

December 5, 1961, suspended proceedings on the merits or issues introduced by South Africa. In accordance with the Statute of the Court, Article 31, South Africa appointed a judge *ad hoc*, the Honorable J. T. van Wyk, judge of the Appellate Division of the Supreme Court of South Africa; Liberia and Ethiopia chose Sir Louis Mbanefo, Chief Justice of the Eastern Region of Nigeria, as judge *ad hoc*. Significantly, this was the first time that jurists from the African continent south of the Sahara region had been seated on the World Court bench.

South Africa in its introductory objections contended that Ethiopia and Liberia had no solid basis for being respondents in the proceedings for the following reasons: 1) the mandate agreement has never been, nor has been since the dissolution of the League of Nations, considered a treaty within the meaning of Article 37 of the World Court Statute, 2) for the reason cited above, then neither Ethiopia nor Liberia was "another member of the League of Nations", 3) Ethiopia and Liberia have no material or nationals (citizens) involved in the dispute, and 4) this alleged dispute or disagreement could be settled by negotiation. Thus, the answer to objections numbers 1 and 2 would depend on the impact of the dissolution of the old League of Nations (1946), the mandate, and Article 7 particularly applying to the mandate system; number 3 objection would be related to the scope and interpretation of Article 7 and mandates; and the answer to number 4 would be construed in light of the fact that no direct negotiations had ever taken place between the applicant (South Africa) and the respondent states (Liberia and Ethiopia) involving basic interpretation of the relevant part of Article 7, mandates.

The Court answered South Africa's objections by stating the following arguments: The Court rejected South Africa's first objection by construing the mandate and its system as a treaty rather than as an executive action of the old League of Nations. The Court relied heavily on its own advisory opinion of 1950, which held that, even though the dissolution of the League of Nations had occurred in 1946, the mandate did survive and that, as a result of the mandate surviving with its attendant responsibilities, South Africa was bound to accept the United Nations in a supervisory function. Also, the Court contended that, with regard to Article 37 of the Court statute, Article 7 of the mandate and its system must still be regarded to be in effect or force; and, as a consequence of this obligation and responsibility, South Africa must accept the compulsory jurisdiction of the World Court.

The Court rejected South Africa's second objection for essentially the same reason cited above. Furthermore, the Court cited the statement by South Africa at a plenary meeting of the old League Assembly on April 9, 1946, that South Africa would "regard the dissolution of the League as in no way diminishing its obligations under the Mandate". The Court also took note of the resolution of the League Assembly adopted unanimously on April 18, 1946, which took "note of the expressed intentions of the members of the League now administering territories under Mandate to continue to administer them for the well-being and development of the peoples concerned in accordance with the obligations contained in the respective Mandates until other arrangements have been agreed between the United Nations and the respective mandatory Powers". The Court concluded its second contention by stating that it considered judicial protection as an essential part of the supervisory system for the mandated territory to ensure its being administered as "a sacred trust of civilization".

The Court dismissed the third objection of South Africa in view of the comprehensive coverage embodied in Article 7 of the Mandate, stating "any dispute whatever". The Court construed this to embody disputes involving the mandatory, and the mandatory's obligations to the League, individual League members, and the inhabitants of the territory mandated.

The fourth objection of South Africa was rejected by the Court on the basis that negotiation or arbitration could never develop on the basis of the attitudes and views of the parties involved. All the parties involved knew that the issues had been explored extensively by the U. N. General Assembly and resolutions cited, as well as Court advisory opinions; all parties involved had been participants in these developments and no direct negotiation or diplomatic relations had developed from these involvements. Thus, the Court dismissed the fourth objection of South Africa.

The World Court rendered a split decision of 8 to 7 in favor of South Africa.

NOTE:

The World Court was profoundly divided by the issues of this case, and the decision of 8 to 7 (finally rendered in September 1966) was a classic. Interestingly enough, the judgment only occupies 32 pages, the concurring individual opinions cover 100 pages, and the dissenting opinions encompass 214 pages. Altogether this case produced a greater volume of judicial reasoning than any other case previously decided by the World Court or its predecessor, the Permanent Court of the old League of Nations.

(See Appendix II for further information concerning this case, pp. 117, 118, 135, and 136.)

Appendix I
CHARTS, MAPS & DIAGRAMS

TIME LINE

Ca. 1900 B.C. Hammurabi's Code
Ca. 1372 B.C. Tel-el-Amarna (Letters from Ikhnaton to Fertile Crescent)
Ca. 1225 B.C. Decalogue or Ten Commandments
Ca. 776 B.C. Olympic Games begin (Law of Hellenes)
Ca. 546 B.C. Peloponnesian League
Ca. 478 B.C. Delian League
Ca. 444 B.C. Law of Twelve Tablets (Rome)
Ca. 330 B.C. *jus gentium* and *jus natural*
Ca.   29 A.D. Sermon on the Mount
       529 A.D. Code Justinian
       800 A.D. Holy Roman Empire
       990 A.D. Peace of God (sacred places free from attack)
      1025 A.D. Truce of God (limited medieval warfare)
Ca. 1050 A.D. Tablet of Amalfi
      1215 A.D. Magna Carta
Ca. 1250 A.D. Code of Barcelona
Ca. 1250 A.D. Code of Wisby
Ca. 1250 A.D. Code of Hansa
Ca. 1260 A.D. St. Thomas Aquinas (*Summa Theologica*)
Ca. 1300 A.D. Code of Oleron
      1620   Mayflower Compact
      1625   *On the Laws of War and Peace* (Groitus)
      1648   Treaties of Westphalia
      1689   Bill of Rights - England
      1776   Declaration of Independence
      1815   Congress of Vienna (Concert of Europe)
      1856   Peace of Paris (piracy on high seas)
      1863   Emancipation Proclamation
      1878 & 1885 - Congresses of Berlin
      1899 & 1907 - Hague Conferences

1905	American Society of International Law
1918	Wilson's 14 Points
1919	Versailles Treaties - Covenant of League of Nations
1921-22	Washington Arms Conference
1925	Locarno Pact
1928	Pact of Paris (Kellogg-Briand)
1938	Munich Pact
1941	Atlantic Charter
1945	Charter of U. N. and London Agreement (August 8, 1945)
1946-48	Nuremberg and Tokyo War Crime Trials
1948	Declaration of Human Rights - Genocide Convention
1950	U. N. (Uniting for Peace) adopted
1951	U. S. - Japanese Treaty negotiations
1957	*Sputnik*
1958-60	Geneva Disarmament negotiations (U-2)
1961	Berlin Wall
1962	Cuba Blockade
1963	A-Test Ban Treaty (American-British-Soviet)
1966	*Ethipia and Liberia v. Southwest Africa*

SOURCES of INTERNATIONAL LAW

Diagrams and Skeletal Source Charts

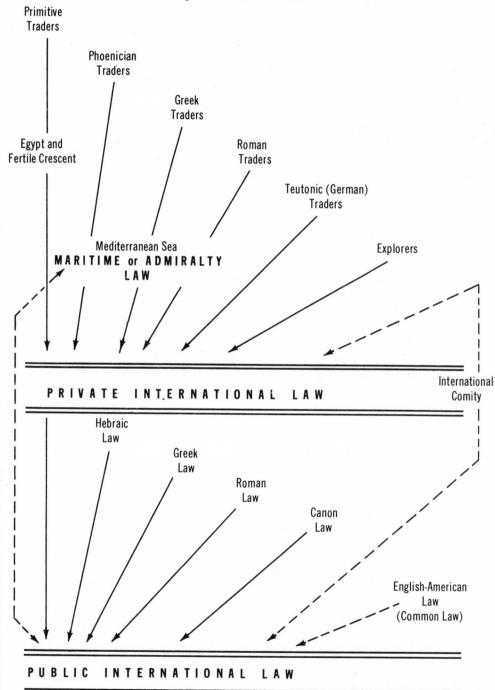

THREE SOURCES *of* INTERNATIONAL LAW

PROBLEMS

CUSTOM

1. Rule or law must be proved by recourse to all sources listed

TREATIES

1. Varying interpretations
2. Degree of acceptance by sovereign states; percentage of consensus to produce law-making effect and use
3. Secret diplomacy and alliances
4. Power relationships may shift and abrogate treaties (expect too much)

GENERAL PRINCIPLES

1. National sovereignty
2. Domestic jurisdiction (conflict of laws)
3. Science and technocracy
4. Outer Space
5. Unequal power of states (Force)

PROBLEM AREAS

1. sovereignty
2. recognition
3. equality of states
4. nationalism
5. nation-state system
6. interdependence - world community - air space
7. isolation - participation
8. national self-help by use of force
9. national self-interest and reciprocity
10. peace, law, justice, security, dignity of man
11. independence - existence
12. consent of state and obligation - jurisdiction - integrity

THREE MAJOR SOURCES of INTERNATIONAL LAW

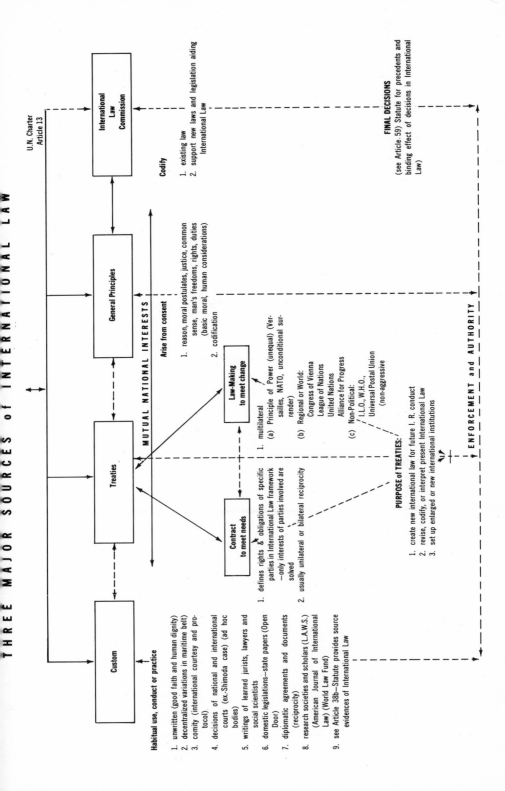

U.N. Charter
Article 13

Custom ← → **Treaties** ← → **General Principles** ← → **International Law Commission**

MUTUAL NATIONAL INTERESTS

Custom

Habitual use, conduct or practice

1. unwritten (good faith and human dignity)
2. decentralized variations in maritime belt)
3. comity (international courtesy and protocol).
4. decisions of national and international courts (ex.-Shimoda case) (ad hoc bodies)
5. writings of learned jurists, lawyers and social scientists
6. domestic legislations—state papers (Open Door)
7. diplomatic agreements and documents (reciprocity)
8. research societies and scholars (L.A.W.S.) (American Journal of International Law) (World Law Fund)
9. see Article 38b—Statute provides source evidences of International Law

Treaties

Contract to meet needs

1. defines rights & obligations of specific parties in International Law framework —only interests of parties involved are solved
2. usually unilateral or bilateral reciprocity

Law-Making to meet change

1. multilateral
   (a) Principle of Power (unequal) (Versailles, NATO, unconditional surrender)
   (b) Regional or World:
       Congress of Vienna
       League of Nations
       United Nations
       Alliance for Progress
   (c) Non-Political:
       I.L.O., W.H.O.,
       Universal Postal Union
       (non-aggressive)

PURPOSE of TREATIES:

1. create new international law for future I. R. conduct
2. revise, codify, or interpret present international law
3. set up enlarged or new international institutions

General Principles

Arise from consent

1. reason, moral postulates, justice, common sense, man's freedoms, rights, duties (basic moral, human considerations)
2. codification

International Law Commission

Codify

1. existing law
2. support new laws and legislation aiding International Law

FINAL DECISIONS

(see Article. 59) Statute for precedents and binding effect of decisions in International Law)

ENFORCEMENT and AUTHORITY

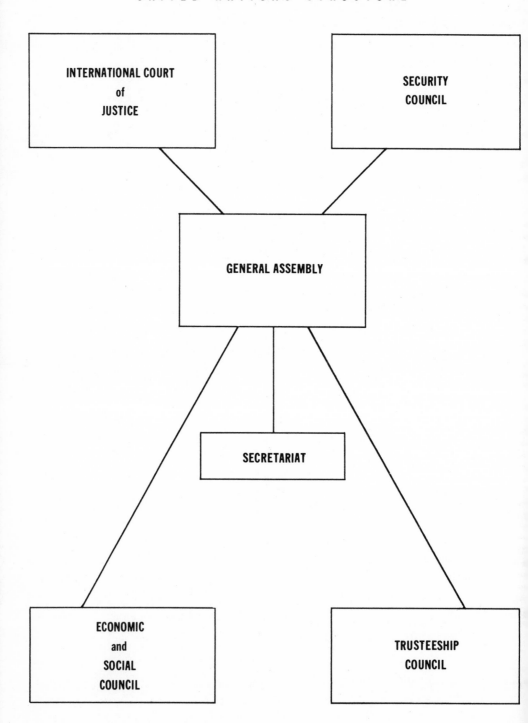

ARTICLE 38 (SOURCES)

Article 38 states that the Court shall apply:

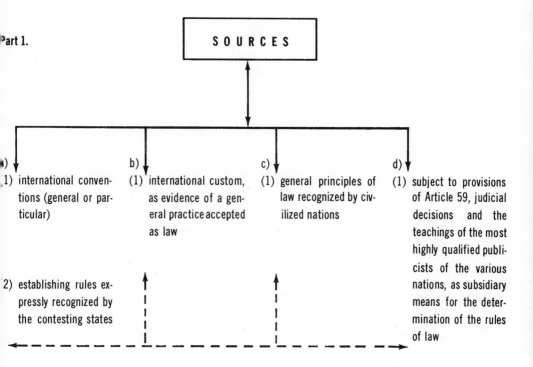

Part 1.

SOURCES

a)
(1) international conventions (general or particular)

(2) establishing rules expressly recognized by the contesting states

b)
(1) international custom, as evidence of a general practice accepted as law

c)
(1) general principles of law recognized by civilized nations

d)
(1) subject to provisions of Article 59, judicial decisions and the teachings of the most highly qualified publicists of the various nations, as subsidiary means for the determination of the rules of law

★Note: Section (d) merely indicates the methods of means by which sections (b) or (c) may be evaluated and determined.

★Note: Article 59 states "that the decision of the Court has no binding force except between the parties and and in respect of that particular case".

Part 2. States that this provision (Article 59) **Statute** shall not prejudice the power of the Court to decide a case **ex aequo et bono** (from a clear, reasoned mind without prejudice), if the parties agree thereto.

THE INTERNATIONAL COURT OF JUSTICE

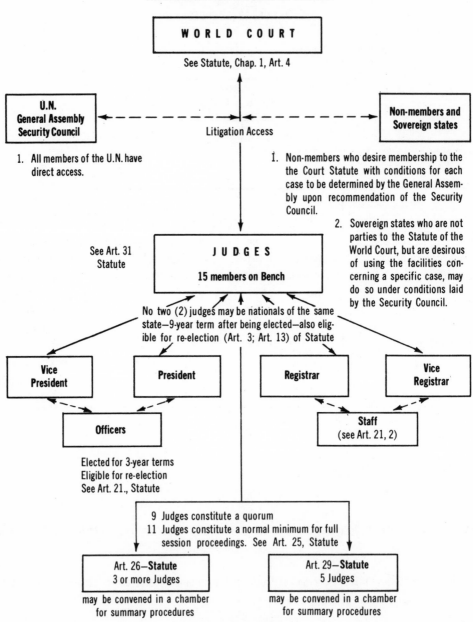

WORLD COURT

See Statute, Chap. 1, Art. 4

U.N. General Assembly Security Council

Litigation Access

Non-members and Sovereign states

1. All members of the U.N. have direct access.

1. Non-members who desire membership to the the Court Statute with conditions for each case to be determined by the General Assembly upon recommendation of the Security Council.

2. Sovereign states who are not parties to the Statute of the World Court, but are desirous of using the facilities concerning a specific case, may do so under conditions laid by the Security Council.

See Art. 31 Statute

JUDGES

15 members on Bench

No two (2) judges may be nationals of the same state—9-year term after being elected—also eligible for re-election (Art. 3; Art. 13) of Statute

Vice President

President

Registrar

Vice Registrar

Officers

Staff (see Art. 21, 2)

Elected for 3-year terms
Eligible for re-election
See Art. 21., Statute

9 Judges constitute a quorum
11 Judges constitute a normal minimum for full session proceedings. See Art. 25, Statute

Art. 26—Statute
3 or more Judges

may be convened in a chamber for summary procedures

Art. 29—Statute
5 Judges

may be convened in a chamber for summary procedures

MEANS TO ACHIEVE
INTERNATIONAL LAW, ETHICS,
MORALITY and JUSTICE

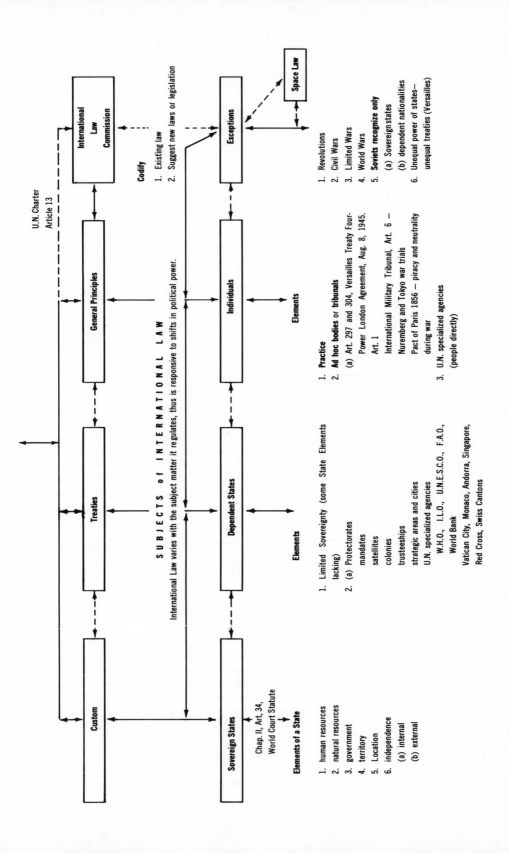

U.N. Charter
Article 13

International Law Commission

Codify
1. Existing law
2. Suggest new laws or legislation

General Principles

Treaties

Custom

Chap. II, Art, 34,
World Court Statute

SUBJECTS of INTERNATIONAL LAW

International Law varies with the subject matter it regulates, thus is responsive to shifts in political power.

Exceptions

Space Law

1. Revolutions
2. Civil Wars
3. Limited Wars
4. World Wars
5. **Soviets recognize only**
   (a) Sovereign states
   (b) dependent nationalities
6. Unequal power of states—
   unequal treaties (Versailles)

Individuals

Elements

1. **Practice**
2. **Ad hoc bodies or tribunals**
   (a) Art. 297 and 304, Versailles Treaty Four-
       Power London Agreement, Aug. 8, 1945.
       Art. 1
       International Military Tribunal, Art. 6 —
       Nuremberg and Tokyo war trials
       Pact of Paris 1856 — piracy and neutrality
       during war
3. U.N. specialized agencies
   (people directly)

Dependent States

Elements

1. Limited Sovereignty (some State Elements lacking)
2. (a) Protectorates
       mandates
       satellites
       colonies
       trusteeships
       strategic areas and cities
       U.N. specialized agencies
       W.H.O., I.L.O., U.N.E.S.C.O., F.A.O.,
       World Bank
       Vatican City, Monaco, Andorra, Singapore,
       Red Cross, Swiss Cantons

Sovereign States

Elements of a State

1. human resources
2. natural resources
3. government
4. territory
5. Location
6. independence
   (a) internal
   (b) external

INTERNATIONAL LAW

Relation to
United States Law

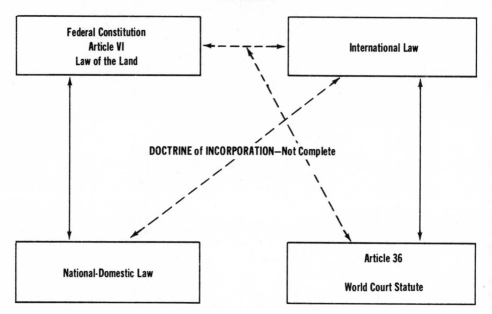

```
┌─────────────────────────┐              ┌─────────────────────────┐
│   Federal Constitution  │ ◄ ─ ─ ─ ─ ►  │                         │
│       Article VI        │              │    International Law    │
│     Law of the Land     │              │                         │
└─────────────────────────┘              └─────────────────────────┘

            DOCTRINE of INCORPORATION—Not Complete

┌─────────────────────────┐              ┌─────────────────────────┐
│                         │              │        Article 36       │
│  National-Domestic Law  │              │                         │
│                         │              │    World Court Statute  │
└─────────────────────────┘              └─────────────────────────┘
```

AMERICAN PRACTICE: CASES

1. **Whitney v. Robertson, 1888**
   Briggs, **op. cit.,** p. 888
2. **Paquette Habana, 1900**
   Briggs, pp. 30-32
3. **Over-the-Top-Case, 1925**
   Kelsen, **op. cit.,** pp. 421, 423, and pp. 567 and 576 (1966 edition)
4. **Hines v. Davidowitz, et al., 1941**
   Briggs, **op. cit.,** p. 538

Thus, American practice tends to support International Law in the majority of instances; however, U.S. Constitution (Article VI) is the common denominator.

NOTE: CONNALLY AMENDMENT, 1946: When the United States accepted the compulsory jurisdiction under the Optional Clause of Article 36 of the Court Statute, it was done so under a Senate Resolution of August 2, 1946, and contained a qualification known as the "Connally Amendment". This amendment restricted the jurisdiction of the Permanent Court of International Justice by stating "that disputes with regard to matters which are essentially within the domestic jurisdiction of the U.S.A. as determined by the U.S.A. shall not apply to the World Court".

SHIMODA v. JAPAN

Dec. 7, 1963

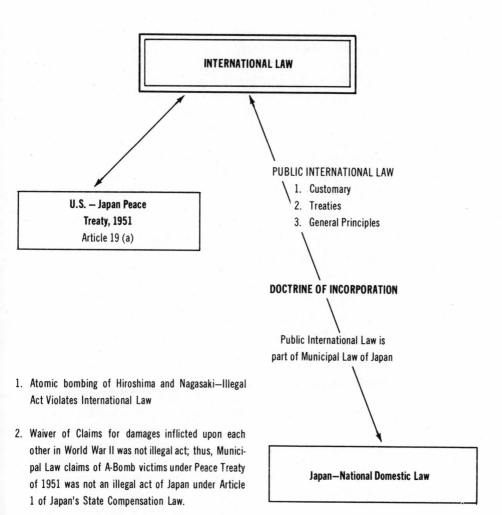

INTERNATIONAL LAW

U.S. – Japan Peace Treaty, 1951
Article 19 (a)

PUBLIC INTERNATIONAL LAW
1. Customary
2. Treaties
3. General Principles

DOCTRINE OF INCORPORATION

Public International Law is part of Municipal Law of Japan

Japan—National Domestic Law

1. Atomic bombing of Hiroshima and Nagasaki—Illegal Act Violates International Law

2. Waiver of Claims for damages inflicted upon each other in World War II was not illegal act; thus, Municipal Law claims of A-Bomb victims under Peace Treaty of 1951 was not an illegal act of Japan under Article 1 of Japan's State Compensation Law.

3. Japan, in upholding the Doctrine of Incorporation and recognizing International Law as part of their Municipal Law, provides for individual claims for redress under their unified inclusiveness.

121

SHIMODA v. JAPAN

WAIVER of CLAIMS:
1. Article 19 (a) of the Japanese Peace Treaty provides that: "Japan waives all claims of Japan and its nationals against the Allied Powers and their nationals arising out of the war or out of actions taken because of the existence of a state of war." Japan has waived the claims in municipal law, as well as the claims in international law against the United states and President Truman. Consequently, the plaintiffs legally have completely lost the claims for damages against the United States and President Truman.
2. The defendant State alleges that it cannot waive the claims of its nationals since the State of Japan is different from the nationals of Japan in personality. Even if there is logical room for such a point of view, the plaintiff's claims for damages will not be permitted by article 19 (a) of the Japanese Peace Treaty, since a treaty has the full force of law in the United States. Further, for the above reason, if the plaintiffs file a suit in the United States, they cannot easily obtain the cooperation of lawyers or the support of public opinion of the United States. It is even extremely difficult to find cooperators in Japan. Therefore, the plaintiffs' instituting a suit is almost impossible actually, and we may safely say that the plaintiffs have lost their claims.

STATE COMPENSATION LAW:
Kokka Baisho Ho, Law No. 125 of October 27, 1947. "Article 1. (1) If an official or servant of the state or a public body intentionally or negligently commits an unlawful act and injures another in the course of performing his duties, the state or the public body is liable to make compensation therefor. (2) In the case of the preceding paragraph (not stated herein), if there has been intent or gross negligence, the state or the public body may claim compensation from the official or servant involved."

JAPANESE CONSITUTION:
Nihon Koku Kempo, November 3, 1947. "Article 29. (1) The right to own or hold property is inviolable. (2) Property rights shall be defined by law, in conformity with the public welfare. (3) Private property may be taken for public use upon just compensation therefor."

FIGURES of PLAINTIFF (Shimoda and Others)—EXHIBIT I

Damaged District	Population prior to Damage	Casualties	
Hiroshima	413,889	Killed:	260,000
		Missing:	6,738
		Seriously wounded:	51,012
		Slightly wounded:	105,543
		Total:	423,293
Nagasaki	280,542	Killed:	73,884
		Wounded:	76,796
		Total:	150,680

FIGURES of DEFENDANT (Japanese Government)—EXHIBIT II

Damaged District	Population prior to Damage	Casualties	
Hiroshima	336,483 (1944)	Killed:	78,150
		Wounded:	51,408
Nagasaki	270,063 (1944)	Killed:	23,753
		Wounded:	41,847

RECOGNITION

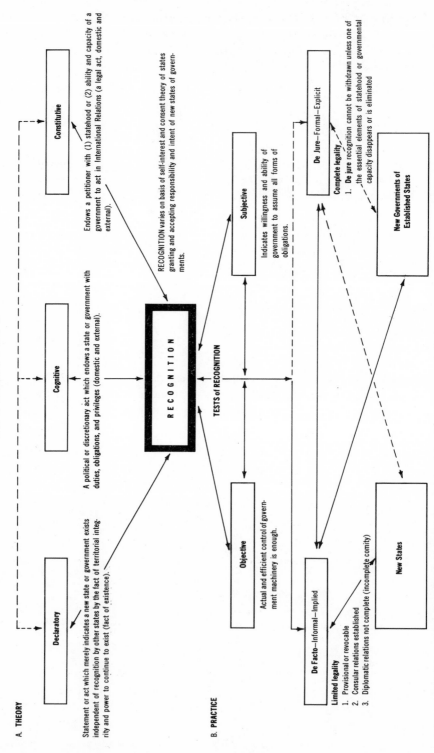

A. THEORY

Declaratory

Statement or act which merely indicates a new state or government exists independent of recognition by other states by the fact of territorial integrity and power to continue to exist (fact of existence).

Cognitive

A political or discretionary act which endows a state or government with duties, obligations, and privileges (domestic and external).

Constitutive

Endows a petitioner with (1) statehood or (2) ability and capacity of a government to act in International Relations (a legal act, domestic and external).

RECOGNITION

RECOGNITION varies on basis of self-interest and consent theory of states granting and accepting responsibility and intent of new states of governments.

TESTS of RECOGNITION

Objective

Actual and efficient control of government machinery is enough.

Subjective

Indicates willingness and ability of government to assume all forms of obligations.

De Facto—Informal—Implied

Limited legality
1. Provisional or revocable
2. Consular relations established
3. Diplomatic relations not complete (incomplete comity)

De Jure—Formal—Explicit

Complete legality
1. De jure recognition cannot be withdrawn unless one of the essential elements of statehood or governmental capacity disappears or is eliminated

New States

New Governments of Established States

B. PRACTICE

1. New government of a new state is automatically recognized—single all-encompassing act. Sovereignty is is recognized and supported against claimants (external and internal).

1. The State remains the same recognized international person, but official relations with other states are not possible until new government is recognized de jure or de facto.

RECOGNITION - PROBLEMS

NEW STATES - complex - usually involves two governments as claimants who do not have identical claims: one government claims it represents a unified territory and people not previously recognized; the other claimant, a government of an existing state, still claiming it has sovereign control over the people and unified territory in question.

EXTENT of RECOGNITION is determined by applying any of the three theoretical means and the practical tests of recognition; objective and subjective, explicit and implicit, historical doctrines and their application and interpretation, and *de jure* or *de facto* status.

NON-RECOGNITION is a political act by an existing state directed against the administration, the government, or a unified territory or people itself seeking acceptance and obligations, but recognition is withheld because the existing state indicates they are not entitled to be recognized due to actions or attitudes abhorrent to our modern standards of civilization.

NEW GOVERNMENTS of EXISTING STATES - usually involves deciding between two claimants making identical claims to represent a unified territory and people. Recognition of one government establishes that government's assumption of its predecessor's obligations and duties. There is only limited recognition of a new government in an established state when this new government has assumed control by violation of recognized procedures: insurgency, belligerency, open intervention, occupancy, annexation.

RECOGNITION HAS INVOLVED NATIONAL COURTS and has generally been construed to be a political question, involving another agency of government—namely, the State Department—and generally is not a juridicial matter. *Comity, the consent of state, conflict of laws, treaties, non-recognition, executive acts, sovereignty, insurgency* and *obligations created*—all have been examined in national courts.

REASONS for DE FACTO STATUS

1. revolutionary origin
2. unstable or not too responsible
3. will not or cannot fulfill international or domestic obligation satisfactorily (loss of legal control and effectiveness)
4. insurgency, belligerency or catastrophic events (act of nature) (loss of people or territory)
5. Note: legal rights and obligations may be created by an illegal act.

★Note: Distinction between governments and states is founded upon the legal purpose of making the obligations of a state binding and insulated from changes in governments of that state.

- -

19th CENTURY

Shifts in territory and population affects both states and governments from an individual and collective basis. National self-interest and the goal of advantage would determine the actions of the individual and collective groups involved. Basis for action then was internal order and stability, and the international norms were implemented upon the acceptance and responsibility of the states' obligations and their ultimate attempts at fulfillment. Europe was at her Apogee from 1815-1914. (Stability, order, responsibility, state obligations and norms of behavior dominated scene. "Balance of power factors".)

20th CENTURY

This century has rocked the 19th century concepts supporting the "balance of power". Shifts in territory and population affects states, governments, and the beginning, continuity, and termination of them.

WEST _ _ _ _ _ _ _ _ _ _ _ _ _ _ _ _ _ _ EAST
NEUTRALIST

Today in our tri-polarized world international norms have been proliferated. Each bloc has its own criteria for behavior, and within individual blocs there are variations. Cynicism, collective security, appeasement, blocs and alliances, **ad hoc** bodies, and the "balance of terror" dominate. Today, recognition by individual states is purely a political matter and not subject to legal norms or criteria, as was the 19th century concept of the balance of power.

126

Appendix II
TREATIES, NOTES AND DOCUMENTS

Territorial Jurisdiction

JOHN BASSETT MOORE, J., on TERRITORIAL JURISDICTION

from his dissenting opinion in the

LOTUS CASE

1. It is an admitted principle of international law that a nation possesses and exercises within its own territory an absolute and exclusive jurisdiction, and that any exception to this right must be traced to the consent of the nation, either express or implied. The benefit of this principle equally enures to all independent and sovereign States and is attended with a corresponding responsibility for what takes place within the national territory.

2. It is an equally admitted principle that, as municipal courts, the creatures of municipal law derive their jurisdiction from that law, offenses committed in the territorial jurisdiction of a nation may be tried and punished there according to the definitions and penalties of its municipal law, which, except so far as it may be shown to be contrary to international law, is accepted by international law as the law properly governing the case. This principle is not contrary, but is correlative, to the principle laid down in numerous decisions of municipal courts, that international law is to be considered as forming part of the law of the land, that it is as such to be judicially administered in all cases to which it is applicable, and that municipal enactments ought not be so construed as to violate international law, if any other construction is possible.

3. The principle of absolute and exclusive jurisdiction within the national territory applies to foreigners as well as to citizens or inhabitants of the country, and the foreigner can claim no exemption from the exercise of such jurisdiction, except so far as he may be able to show either: (1) that he is, by reason of some special immunity, not subject to the operation of the local law, or (2) that the local law is not in conformity with international law. No presumption of immunity arises from the fact that the person accused is a foreigner. . . .

It is well settled that a State is bound to use due diligence to prevent the commission within its dominions of criminal acts against another nation or its people.

TERMS

nation

state

nation-state system

sovereignty

national self-interest

national self-help

act of state

sovereign immunity

doctrine of incorporation

diplomatic protection

litigation

procedural law

substantive law

particular law

universal law

positive law

natural law

customary law

conventional law

law of reciprocity (comity)

law of coordination

theory of consent (state
binds itself)

duress of unequal power

treaties (law-making and
contract)

domestic jurisdiction

conflict of laws

world community

regionalism

blocs

sanction

reprisal

outer space

morality

interdependence

individual and collective
responsibility

moral norms

jural or legal norms

international rights

international legislation

isolationism

imperialism

alliances

accord

boycott

jus gentium

jus natural

national armaments

defendant

plaintiff

human rights

war crimes

genocide

ad hoc bodies

reparations

balance of terror

power politics

continuity of international
obligations

statute of limitations

unilateral agreements

bilateral agreements

multilateral agreements

aggression

hegemony

autonomy

non-intervention

neutrality

coercion

ultimatum

tariff

embargo

diplomacy

obligations

decentralized law
recognition
private international law
public international law
equality and universal
  brotherhood of man
plenipotentiaries
ratifications
in rem
boycott
pacific blockade
inter alia
good offices
retorsion
constitutive
declaratory
belligerent
blockade
semi-independent
accretion
western colonialism
de jure

succession rights
balance of power
government
prescription
Connally Amendment
self-determination
security
spheres of influence
human rights a domestic
  problem

discovery
adjudication
dynastic legitimacy
creditor nation
appeasement
bipolar blocs

sanctions - criminal and civil
the *delict*
culpability
absolute responsibility
retribution
prevention
bellum justum

inquiry commissions
cognitive
neutral
pogroms (Ukraine, 1903, 1905,
  1917-27)
insurgent
expulsion (deportation)
occupation
universal jurisdiction
passive-personality principle
Vatican visa (Eichmann)
de facto
customary rights
continuity of state
law of state succession
internal order
conquest
Calvo Clause
stability
probation
norms of the international
  system
extraterritoriality (territorial
  rights)
prestige
cession
coup d'etat
debtor nation
collective security
new norms—ideological and
  political
uncommitted states

EVENTS or AREAS	DOCTRINES OF RECOGNITION
Esthonia)	Jefferson 1792
Latvia) Ghost States	Tobar 1907
Lithuania)	Wilson 1913
Latin American Revolts 1810-25	Estrada 1930
Congress of Vienna 1815	Stimson 1932
Concert of Europe 1815-22	
Ottoman Empire (Turkey)	CASES
Greece 1827	
Crimean War 1854-56	*Armenian Tindelian Case 1921*
German-Italian Unification 1871	(Berlin)
Congress of Berlin 1878	*Shalom Schwartzbard Case 1926*
Congress of Berlin 1885	(Paris)
Dreyfuss Affair 1894-98	*Berthold Jacob Case 1935*
Secession of Panama from	(Kidnapped from Switzerland
Colombia - led to our	by Gestapo)
Canal Zone 1903	
League of Nations 1919	
Pact of Paris 1928 (Kellogg-	
Briand)	
Mukden Incident 1931	
Italy vs. Ethiopia 1935	
Spanish Civil War 1936-39	
Marco Polo Bridge Incident 1937	
Austria 1938	
Wansee Conference 1942 (Berlin)	
Nuremberg War Trials 1945-46	
Nationalist China 1949	
Red China 1949	
Korea 1950	
French-Indo China 1954	
Algeria 1954	
Suez 1956	
African States 1955-1961	
Vietnam & Southeast Asia 1954-66	

PEOPLE

Francisco de Vittoria (1480-1546)
Albericus Gentilis (1522-1608)
Francisco Suarez (1548-1617)
Hugo Grotius (1583-1645)
Thomas Hobbes (1588-1679)
Richard Zouche (1590-1660)
Samuel Pufendorf (1632-1694)
Benedict Spinoza (1634-1677)
Cornelius Van Bynkershock (1673-1743)
Christian Wolff (1676-1756)
Lord Stowell (1745-1836)
Jeremy Bentham (1748-1832)
James Kent (1763-1847)
George W. F. Hegel (1770-1831)
John Austin (1790-1859)
Francis Lieber (1800-1872)
David D. Field (1805-1894)
Pasquale Fiore (1837-1914)
Woodrow Wilson (1856-1924)
Frank B. Kellogg (1856-1937)
John Bassett Moore (1860-1947)
Charles Evans Hughes (1862-1948)
Franklin D. Roosevelt (1882-1945)
Manley O. Hudson (1886-1960)
Adolf Hitler (1889-1945)
Robert H. Jackson (1892-   )
*Philipp C. Jessup
Charles de Visscher
Dr. Robert Servatius
Richard Klement (Eichmann)

*Present U. S. Justice on World Court Bench - Term expires 1970

SOME CONSTITUTIONAL PROVISIONS FOR
USE OF INTERNATIONAL LAW

GERMANY, BASIC LAW FOR THE FEDERAL REPUBLIC OF GERMANY, THE "BONN CONSTITUTION" 1949

Article 25. The general rules of international law shall form part of federal law. They shall take precedence over the laws and create rights and duties directly for the inhabitants of the federal territory.*

ITALY, CONSTITUTION of 1948

Article 10. The Italian juridicial system conforms to the generally recognized principles of international law.

      The juridicial status of the foreigner is regulated by law in conformity with international rules and treaties. . .

*Cf. Article 4 of the German Constitution of 1919 (Weimar): "The generally recognized rules of international law are binding as constituent parts of the law of the German Reich." Comparable provisions were incorporated in Article 9 of the Austrian Constitution of 1920, Article 4 of the Estonian Constitution of 1920, and Article 7 of the Spanish Constitution of 1931.

Article 5 of the Draft Constitution for East (Communist) Germany (1949) provided: "The generally recognized principles of international law shall be binding upon the sovereign State and its citizens. . ." No comparable provisions appear in the constitutions of other Soviet satellites.

RECORDED VOTES OF THE
INTERNATIONAL COURT OF JUSTICE

LIBERIA and ETHIOPIA v. SOUTH AFRICA, 1960-66

Vote of International Court in favor of South Africa

MAJORITY – 8	MINORITY – 7
Australia (2 votes)	Nationalist China
Poland	United States
Greece	U. S. S. R.
Great Britain	Mexico
Italy	Senegal
France	Japan
South Africa	Nigeria

NOTE: In 1960 when this case was brought to the International Court, the case was initiated and based upon the so-called "compromissary clause" of Article 7 of the mandate. The clause reads as follows and states:

> "The Mandatory agrees that, if any dispute whatever should arise between the Mandatory and another member of the League of Nations relating to the interpretation or the application of the provisions of the Mandate, such dispute, if it cannot be settled by negotiation, shall be submitted to the Permanent Court of International Justice. . ."

135

INTERNATIONAL COURT OF JUSTICE

1966

(The Court seat is The Hague, Netherlands)

PRESIDENT: Sir Percy Spender, Australia (1967)
VICE PRESIDENT: V. K. Wellington Koo, Nationalist China (1967)
Jose Luis Bustamente y Rivero, Peru (1970)
Sir Gerald Fitzmaurice, United Kingdom (1973)
Isaac Forster, Senegal (1973)
Andre Gros, France (1973)
*Phillip C. Jessup, U. S. A. (1970)
Sri Muhammed Zafrulla Khan, Pakistan (1973)
Vladimir M. Koretsky, U. S. S. R. (1970)
Gaetano Morelli, Italy (1970)
Luis Padilla Nervo, Mexico (1973)
Jean Spiropoulos, Greece (1967)
Kotaro Tanaka, Japan (1970)
Bohdan Winiarski, Poland (1967)
*Vacancy (1967) caused by death of Abdil Hamid
Badawi, U. A. R.

The Court is composed of 15 Judges who serve 9-year terms and may be re-elected.

Expiration dates are in parentheses. All terms expire February 5 of the year designated.

GLOSSARY OF TERMS

From the long list of terms compiled on pages 127 and 128, the following identifications have been chosen, added to, and defined as an aid to the student and the teacher. Some teachers feel that certain terms may not be adequately explained in a few words and that is the duty of the instructor to enlarge and clarify these unusual words and phrases; however, the vast consensus of teachers will agree that students should consult reference works, seek aid from the librarians in pursuit of the needed reference works, and avail themselves of unabridged dictionaries as often as possible.

ABROGATE ....to annul or break
AD HOC ....deals with a single case or issue
ADMIRALTY COURT ....jurisdiction over maritime questions
ASYLUM....................................protection provided to political refugees by a foreign government
AUTARCHY ....economic self-sufficiency
BELLIGERENT ....a nation engaged in war
BELLIGERENCY ....a state of war exists between two or more states
BENEVOLENT NEU-
   TRALITY ....neutral, but favors one side
CARTEL ....an international monolopy
CASUS BELLI..........................reason upon which war was justified
COLD WAR................................international struggle; means other than armed combat are used
COLLECTIVE RESPON-
   SIBILITY ....entire group is held responsible for act or acts of its individual members
COMITY.(nations)......................respect, consideration, and understanding among nations or states with regard for each other's institutions and laws

CONSENT of STATES ....to be legally bound by certain norms (moral norms)

CONSORTORIUM ....international banking or business combination

CONTAINMENT ....Communism restricted to fixed territorial limits

COUP D'ETAT..........................quick, forcible overthrow of a government

COURT OF CASSATION ....the highest court of appeal in Fr.

CUSTOMARY INTER-
  NATIONAL LAW.....................refers to diplomatic privileges, immunities, territorial waters, and open seas

DE FACTO ....a government actually functioning, usually after a revolution or *coup*, but not yet permanently recognized or established

DE JURE ....a lawful, fully recognized government, capable of full responsibility; not necessarily emerged from *de facto* status

DEMARCHE..............................diplomatic representation

DENOUNCE..............................public, formal notice which terminates agreement or treaty

DOCTRINE OF CON-
  TINUOUS VOYAGE ....refers to non-contraband cargo and its uninterrupted movement from port of origin to destination

ELAN ....eagerness for action, spirit and ardor

EMBASSY ....residence of an ambassador and his staff

ENVOY.....................................diplomatic courier or official on a special mission

ERSATZ....................................a substitute for the real product; artificial product

EXPATRIATION ....right of a person to change his citizenship

EXPERTISE..............................expert opinion

EXPROPRIATION ....property confiscated by a national government

EXTRADITION ....surrender of a person charged with crime by one nation to another nation

EXTRATERRITORIALITY ....does not free a diplomat from his duty of complying with local law, but does make him immune from local jurisdiction

FACE..prestige of a nation

FAUX PAS ....false or bad step

FILIBUSTER ....an unauthorized armed force led against a friendly nation

FREEDOM of the SEAS ....the right of merchantmen to travel the high seas

FREEZING ....to impound or immobilize assets of a foreign nation or foreign individuals

GENERAL LAW ....refers to law which involves large groups of nations, treaties or blocs

GENOCIDE ....mass extermination of large groups of people

GOOD OFFICES........................a third party offers his services to aid in bringing disputing parties together

HEGEMONY.............................political ascendency of a state over others; preponderance or authority

IDEOLOGY...............................a systematic scheme of ideas for government and society

IMMUNITY (DIPLOMATIC).......foreign envoys are immune from local jurisdiction (comity)

IMPASSE ,...............................a situation in which there is no apparent means to solve the problem

INSURGENCY...........................a seething period of unrest or turmoil with no apparent organized revolutionary government; a state of being just short of full belligerency

INTERNECINE.........................mutual slaughter among a common ethnic group, tribal wars or civil wars

INTERNATIONAL LAW
or LAW of NATIONS...............the body of principles which civilized states regard as binding on

them in their dealings with one another; also decentralized law

INTERVENTION ....to intercede in foreign relations to protect national self-interest

JINGOISM or *CHAUVINISM* ......super-heated patriotism; my country—right or wrong

JURAL NORM ....standards or laws enforceable by organized governments

JUS GENTIUM..........................law of nations

JUS NATURAL..........................natural law or law of nature

JUSTICIABLE...........................a problem recognized as being suitable for adjudication

LAW of COORDINATION...........refers to law which relates to regulation of opium traffic, white slave trade, dependent peoples, and treatment of refugees

LAW of POWER..........................a master-slave relationship

LEGATION..............................the official residence of a diplomatic minister

MEDIATION.............................a third party who is invited in by two disputants to intercede and aid in a solution to the dispute

MODUS VIVENDI ....a temporary arrangement prior to final arrangements

MORAL NORM ....modes of behavior expected by certain groups or nations; matter of conscience

NUNCIO..................................the Ambassador of the Pope at a foreign capital

ORDER in COUNCIL
(BRITISH 19th CENTURY).......an executive order by the Cabinet alone

PAPER BLOCKADE ....an ineffective blockade, written but not stringly enforced

PARTICULAR LAW.....................refers to a specific agreement between states and applied to them only

PLEBISCITE.............................the vote of a people in a given area; usually concerns sovereignty

PLENARY ....full authority for a representative or council to inquire into an issue

140

PLENIPOTENTIARY..................a diplomatic agent clothed with full power to negotiate specific, instructed areas

PUBLIC INTERNATIONAL
LAW...see INTERNATIONAL LAW or LAW of NATIONS

POSITIVE LAW ....volutional law arising from consent; man-made law

POLITY ....the form or constitution of a state; a politically organized body

POWER POLITICS.....................the means by which a nation advances its self-interest in the realm of international relations through superior coercive power

PRIVATE INTERNATIONAL
LAW (CONFLICT OF LAWS)...refers to matters which fall within the jurisdiction of states; it involves individuals, the problem being to determine whose law to apply

PRIZE COURT...........................a court authorized to judge captures at sea during wartime

PROCEDURAL LAW..................refers to methods of specific settlement of problems

PROTOCOL ....the rules of diplomatic etiquette

QUID PRO QUO ....something in return for equal value

RAPPROCHEMENT ....to establish or re-establish cordial relations between powers

RATIFY......................................to make valid or effective

RECIPROCITY, LAW of..............the granting of certain rights to other states in return for rights granted in return (economic)

RECOGNITION ....the recognition of a new government as exercising the powers of a state by entering into formal relations with it; also can pertain to independence, insurgency, and belligerency

REPARATIONS ....payment in money or goods by a state for damages inflicted by that state

REPRISAL ....a retaliatory action by one nation against another nation

RIGHT of VISIT and SEARCH ....the right of a warring nation to search merchantmen on the high seas to determine nationality and cargo

SANCTIONS ....the penalties, usually of an economic or military nature, established for a breach of an international obligation

SHIRT-SLEEVE DIP-
   LOMACY ....unconventional, informal diplomacy

SINE QUA NON.........................an indispensable condition

SOVEREIGNTY..........................supreme rule or power, unrestricted authority of the state

SPHERE of INFLUENCE ....a zone of influence in which one power is permitted by others to exercise almost exclusive influence; see EXTRATERRITORIALITY for enlargement of sphere of influence

STATE.......................................a sovereign power which exercises control over both inhabitants and territory

STATUS QUO ....affairs as they now exist and must continue at present

STATUS QUO ANTE ....to return to affairs as they existed prior to the present state in existence

SUBSTANTIVE LAW...................refers to specific territorial rights of a state

TERRITORIAL WATERS ....the marginal belt of seas included within a state's boundaries

THREE-MILE LIMIT.................the extent traditionally to which a nation's marginal belt extended into the seas (varies now)

TRIAL BALLOON ....a proposal, tentatively put forward to test public reactions and response

ULTIMATE DESTINATION ....final destination of goods, expecially contraband; see the DOCTRINE of CONTINUOUS VOYAGE

ULTIMATUM...............................final terms in negotiation; rejection usually leads to hostility

UNILATERAL............................one-sided action by a group or nation

VATICAN.................................the papal government

VISA.......................................to pass; the bearer's passport is endorsed and the bearer may proceed

Appendix III
EXPERIMENTAL MATERIAL—AMERICAN
DIPLOMATIC EVENTS AND WORLD LAW

TRUMAN BARES 'EARTH-SHAKER'

Beat the Germans to It, He Says:
'Greatest Gamble' Cost 2 Billion

WASHINGTON—(AP)—An atomic bomb, hailed as the most terrible destructive force in history and as the greatest achievement of organized science, has been loosed upon Japan.

President Truman disclosed in a White House statement today that the first use of the bomb—containing more power than 20,000 tons of TNT and producing more than 2,000 times the blast of the most powerful bomb ever dropped before—was made 16 hours earlier on Hiroshima, Japanese army base.

The atomic bomb is the answer, President Truman said, to Japan's refusal to surrender. Secretary of War Stimson predicted the bomb will "prove a tremendous aid" in shortening the Japanese war.

Mr. Truman grimly warned that "even more powerful forms (of the bomb) are in development." He said:

"If they do not now accept our terms, they may expect a rain of ruin from the air the like of which has never been seen on this earth."

* * * * * *

THE WAR DEPARTMENT reported that "an impenetrable cloud of dust and smoke" cloaked Hiroshima after the first atomic bomb crashed down on the city of 318,000 at 6:20 p.m. (Chicago time) yesterday. It was impossible to make an immediate assessment of the damage.

The raid on Hiroshima, located on Honshu Island on the shores of the Inland Sea, had not been disclosed previously, although the 20th Air Force on Guam announced that 580 Superforts raided four Japanese cities at about the same time.

President Truman said he would recommend that Congress consider establishing a commission to control production of atomic power within the United States, adding:

"I shall . . . make . . . recommendations to Congress as to how atomic power can become a powerful and forceful influence toward the maintenance of world peace."

147

Both Mr. Truman and Secretary Stimson, while emphasizing the peacetime potentiality of the new force, made clear that much research must be undertaken to effect full peacetime application of its principles.

* * * * * *

Excerpted from the *Chicago Daily News*, Monday, August 6, 1945

INDEX

INDEX

Act of state doctrine, 104
ad hoc, 62
Adjudication, 32
Albania, 76-78
  Special Agreement of March 25, 1948, 78
Alfonso XIII of Spain, arbitral award by, 88-89
Alien(s),
  certificate of residence, 28-29
  duties to, 68
  registration of, 67, 69-71
  rights of, 53
American Banana Co. v. United Fruit Co., 1909, 36-38
Arbitral award(s), 88-89
Arbitration, 37
Argentina, 91-92
Austria, 91
Averment (positive statement), 51

Banco Nacional de Cuba v. Sabbatino, 1964, 102-104
Belgium, 61,
belligerency, 18-19
Bernadotte and Others, 1949, 81-83
Boundary dispute, 88, 93-95
Breach of contract, 52
Brest-Litovsk, Treaty of, 40
British West Indies, 42

Calvo, Carlos, 53
Calvo Doctrine, The, 53
Cambodia, 93-95
Cambodia v. Thailand, 1962, 93-95
Cameroon, Republic of, 96-97
Cameroon v. United Kingdom, 1963, 96-97
Canada, 26, 62-63
Carrera v. Carrera, 1949, 79-80
Castro, Fidel, 102
certiorari, 74
Chile, 23-24
China, 64-66
  National Government of, 21-22
  Republic of, 21
Chung Chi Cheung v. The King, 1938, 64-66
Civil law, 47
  and diplomatic immunity, 58-59
Claims Commission(s),
  American-Mexican, 53

General, 52-53, 54-55, 56-57
  Mixed, 46-48, 88
  United States—Canada, 62-63
Claims, international, 83
Code Napoleon, 25
Colombia, Republic of, 36-37
Comity, 25, 43, 44, 84, 103
Common law, 46-47
Compensation, 47-49, 63
Condemnation, 33
Congo, Republic of the, 60
Convention of Lausanne (1923), 4
Conversion (unlawful seizure), 43
Coolidge, President Calvin, 22
Corfu Channel Case, 1949, The, 76-78
Costa Rica, 37
Court(s)

  Admiralty, 23, 39, 41,
  of Appeals, 21-22, 30, 39, 41
  Central Criminal, 26
  Circuit, 9, 28-29
  Criminal, 3-4, 23-25
  of Criminal Appeals, 23, 26-27
  District, 9, 90-92, 98, 101
  of International Justice, Permanent, 3, 4-5
  and jurisdiction of, 90-91, 105-106
  Supreme, 9, 28-29, 92, 106
  see also Great Britain; International Court of Justice; United States; and World Court

Cuba, 33, 102-103
Customary law, 11, 13, 27, 61
Czechoslovakia, 79-80

Damages,
  claims for, 99-101
  in death cases, 46-48
de facto, 41, 43, 44
de jure, 43, 44
Demurrer (hesitant action), 60, 66
Denmark, 15
Deportation, 28, 67, 70
Dickinson v. Del Solar, 1929, 58-59
Diplomatic immunity, 58-59, 79-80, 84-85
Diplomatic protection, 99
Diplomatic status, 85
Doctrine of hot pursuit, 63
Doctrine of incorporation, 99, 100-101
Domestic law, 65

154